YOU CAN HAVE IT ALL WITH REAL ESTATE!

How to Harness the Power of the American Dream

Carey Gatto

Open Sesame Productions
Winchester, MA 01890 USA

Typeset by Amnet Systems.

TABLE OF CONTENTS

1

INTRODUCTION

"So much time and so little to see.
Wait a minute. Strike that. Reverse it."

—*Willy Wonka, Charlie and the Glass*
Elevator

After I had my first child, Benjamin, I had 3½ months of paid maternity leave from my job as an assistant to a talent agent. I went back to work full-time after my leave was over. My working hours were 9am to 7pm. I took my newborn to a home daycare near my Beverly Hills office so I could visit him on my lunch breaks. As a new mom, being away from him all day five days a week was utterly traumatic. I missed him so much. Every fiber of my being just wanted to be with my baby. It became my utmost priority to find a way to do just that. I took every second of paid time off that my company offered.

In between hounding studios for payment for our clients and performing other mundane tasks, I furiously Googled work-at-home jobs from my desk. I researched everything from medical transcribing to professional blogging, a fairly new phenomenon at the time. I came close to getting a job as a blogger. Around this time, my dad introduced me to a book called *"Rich Dad, Poor Dad"* by Robert Kyosaki. I had no idea that it was a bestseller, and it was a revelation to me. For once, it became crystal clear that there were good alternatives to working 9 to 5 for someone else (or 9 to 7 in my case). Ultimately, I decided to go into real estate so that I could be my own boss.

Looking back now, I wonder why I was so blindsided by the harsh reality of being a working mother with a young child. Why did I ever think working 9 to 7 would be OK with a new baby? I hadn't put a lot of thought into work-life balance as far as I can remember. I guess I just assumed that a woman has a baby and then returns to her profession and life goes on. That's the way it seemed to always be done. In our equal opportunity society, why wouldn't a woman continue on her career path just like a man would? My upbringing taught me that I could, and should, have it all: the soul-satisfying high-powered career as well as time to raise a family. Isn't that what the whole feminist movement was all about?

Yet having my first baby turned my world upside down. I was unprepared for the transformational love

I felt for Benjamin. I found my priorities completely shifting. My dream of a career in film was superseded by a desire to be a stay-at-home mom, something I had never even considered before. When my son was 9 months old, my husband and I moved from L.A. back to Boston to be closer to our families. We both started new careers that would allow us more flexibility to spend precious time with Benjamin.

I reinvented myself after the birth of my son, and I have continued on that path ever since. Ten years and two more kids later, I do feel that I have it all – a rewarding career that allows me to grow personally and professionally, plus the ability to spend quality time with my family. I am able to live life on my own terms. It's by no means perfect. In fact, it's often messy and very imperfect. However, I have learned to see the perfection in the imperfections, much like a Norman Rockwell painting. And, most importantly, I have the ability to choose.

I can pick my children up from school when they are sick without having to ask permission from a superior. I can go to the school concerts and baseball games, and I can bring my kids to work if I like. I can work a 4-day week or a 6-day week. I can work 7am to 2pm or 3pm to 10pm. I can work at home or from an office. It's up to me, and that's how I like it.

Freedom.

We might not have met yet, however I can guarantee that no one can create the life you want but you. If you want your life to match your values, it's up to you to make it happen. Far too many people I know, both younger and older, are living someone else's life. And they're not happy doing it, even if they won't admit it to themselves.

Why Real Estate?
I believe real estate is a powerful vehicle for creating a life by design because it gives you the opportunity to *create wealth by adding value and by investing in a tangible asset. Rather than just trading time for money, as I used to do, I am building for the future. Time is working for me.*

Time is the most precious commodity we have. If you only trade time for money, you will always have to wake up and do it again. The key to building wealth is to have your money work *for* you by investing, acquiring assets and creating passive income. Even when you are not working, you are still increasing your wealth. There are many ways of getting beyond the "trading time for money" merry-go-round, but for many people real estate is the easiest and the one with the highest payoff.

My intention in writing this book is to give you a basic understanding of how to build long-lasting wealth and financial freedom. I don't know where you are in your financial journey. If you're like me, your schooling included very little financial education, if any at all. Over my ten years in real estate, I have met many folks who have never even considered real estate investment even though it is the most accessible path to building wealth.

These pages are based on my own experience as well as the wisdom I have gained from countless blogs, podcasts, books, seminars, networking events, etc. There are lots of resources available, and my book is by no means the end-all-be-all of real estate investing. But I wrote it because nothing else I came across spoke to young working families in a way that took them from A to Z in the search for the life of their dreams.

Perhaps my book is your starting point in your journey to financial independence – a first glimpse into a whole new way of looking at things. Perhaps it ties together various concepts you have already explored or adds some valuable insights to your existing breadth of knowledge and experience. Maybe it's a gift to a loved one. I would be more than happy with any of these outcomes. My personal mission is to help as many people as possible achieve financial independence. I believe that when we get out of the rat race of trading time for money, we have much better odds of achieving our full potential and purpose in life. This makes us happier and allows us to be better contributors to society.

When I majored in Psychology at Boston College, I learned about Abraham Maslow's Hierarchy of Needs (see the Figure 1 below).

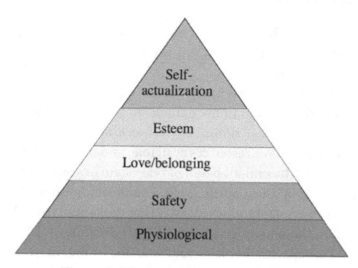

Figure 1. Maslow's Hierarchy of Needs

Maslow said that we work our way up this pyramid. Towards the bottom we have to take care of basic needs such as food, water, shelter, and safety. This is where the cave dwellers resided. Each and every day, they needed to search for food and fend off attacks from predators. When those needs are met with the advent of civilization, the next levels up in the pyramid are psychological and societal needs, for example, a sense of belonging and self-esteem. When those needs are met, humans will next seek self-fulfillment or self-actualization.

As humans, we will naturally strive to achieve our full potential, including creativity, self-expression, and making our mark in the world. Starving artists aside, humans tend to require satisfaction of basic needs before attending to the higher needs of self-actual-ization. This is true especially if we have kids who are dependent on us. We can feel the tug of needing to self-actualize, yet the daily struggle to pay bills and put food on the table often takes precedence because of its immediacy and urgency. It's hard to concentrate on one's own well-being when a screaming child is in the next room.

People can achieve their full potential in a number of ways. It needn't be riches or fame. However, I would argue that wealth certainly helps. Wealth can open doors and free you from the daily grind so you can live your biggest life. Although wealth may not be an end in itself, and it is certainly true that "you can't take it with you," wealth is a means of helping yourself and others. Instead of "the love of money is the root of all evil," Robert Kyosaki says "the lack of money is the root of all evil."

Doesn't a lot of crime come about from the lack of money? As Willie Sutton famously said when asked why he robbed banks, "because that's where the money is." He and so many other criminals stole from others because they lacked money.

On the flip side, I'm sure you have walked into a hospital or a museum and seen a plaque in honor of all the donors who support the organization. That is a reflection of the abundance that those people were able to share with others. What if you could send $100,000 to victims of the next natural disaster without blinking an eye, or help a family member launch an amazing business? When you have more than enough, you can afford to be generous.

According to **Forbes,** Bill Gates gave $4.6 Billion to charity in 2017. Think about the impact that kind of money can make in the world. Churches, schools, universities, hospitals, museums, cancer research – all of them require money. But you don't have to be a billionaire to make a huge impact in the world. When more people have financial stability and abundance, they can then spill into the world around them, much like a tiered fountain that causes a ripple effect. The more people who have the ability to give, even a little bit, the more the world becomes a better place. And the act of giving opens up the giver to receive more and aligns them with their best self. Much like the infinity symbol, the energy you put out comes back to you in an endless cycle of love.

The image below represents my Big Why (see Figure 2). As I help others to become financially abundant and independent, in turn, they are able to live their biggest life and help more people. Helping others is the highest form of self-actualization in my opinion and the purest form of happiness.

As Russell Conwell once wrote, there are acres of diamonds readily available for each of us if we only open ourselves up to the possibilities and opportunities at our feet. We are fortunate to live in a land of opportunity in the U.S. Any man or woman can truly set their sights on a goal, work hard, and bring a dream

Figure 2. Cascading Water Fountain

to fruition. Real estate offers a repeatable and accessible route to wealth, provided that you understand a few basic rules of thumb. If you already know this, you are ahead of the game.

Many of us recognize the benefits of owning a home, yet few of us take the next step of investing in real estate. As a full-time, top-producing real estate agent with a world-class company and an active, experienced investor, I immerse myself in the business daily. I am constantly learning and am eager and enthusiastic to share my knowledge. I invite you to join me on my path to financial independence.

Even though there are many paths and each will be different, the fact remains that more wealthy people in the world have obtained their riches through real estate than with any other vehicle. It is a highly *replicable* path to financial independence. (We all dream of becoming billionaires with the next great start-up, but let's face it, the odds are highly stacked against us.) Two things I love about real estate are 1) it's the only industry I know of where there is literally no ceiling on your income and potential, and 2) anyone can do it as long as they are willing to work hard and give whatever it takes. You don't need a fancy education or specialized training.

Real estate offers the potential to leverage your money and create exponential value on an initial investment. The potential return can be almost infinite. By leveraging your money using financing (mortgages), buying cash-flowing properties and by long-term appreciation, your hard-earned money can well exceed the return of investing in the stock market. Also, you have much more control. When you invest in the stock market, you are effectively investing in other peoples' businesses and hoping they do well. You have little to no control over the failure or success of those companies. However, when you have a real estate portfolio, you make the decisions -- everything from when to improve the properties to when to raise the rents to whom to rent to. This kind of responsibility may seem daunting, especially if you have not yet purchased your first home, yet the fact is anyone can do it! That's the beauty of it. You don't need to be a financial genius or be born wealthy to get started. History abounds with rags to riches stories of people who came from nothing and built fortunes with real estate. In fact, the sooner you get started, the better! As Warren Buffett would say, you are actually losing money by not investing today. When you invest, time works in your favor. So without further ado, let's get into the meat and potatoes, shall we?

2

DO YOU HAVE A FINANCIAL PLAN FOR YOUR LIFE?

"Nature never hurries yet everything is accomplished."

—*Lao Tzu*

I love the above quote from Lao Tzu – everything gets done, but there is no hurry. I know that life isn't always this way, but the saying calms me down. In nature, there is always something happening, something changing. There's so much going on, from photosynthesis to evolution. And yet, nature never hurries. That's because nature has a plan. The plan is ingrained in every cell, in the DNA of every living thing. Then slowly and surely, the plan is executed. A caterpillar becomes a butterfly. A leaf changes color and falls in the autumn. An acorn grows into a massive tree. A baby crawls, then walks.

Most Americans don't have a financial plan beyond just scraping by, which is probably why most Americans live paycheck to paycheck. I'm an artist by nature, and when I was younger, I was kind of a bohemian, not into balancing my checkbook let alone engaging in any kind of financial education. I never wanted to think about money. In fact, it felt beneath me.

I wanted to live in the creative, intuitive world, not fretting over boring things like bank statements, bills, budgets, or stocks. However, I learned over time that by avoiding thinking about money, I was ensuring that I would spend more time worrying about it. Without planning, I ended up living paycheck-to-paycheck and accumulating debt, which meant I was constantly worrying about money. I eventually woke up and realized that in order to have less stress around money, it would require education and then a strategy. So, I bit the bullet and started setting financial goals. I even created a monthly budget, something I never thought I would do.

Ask yourself this question, How much money does *your* desired lifestyle require? Do you even know the answer?

I happen to love traveling. The world has so much to offer, and there are so many things and places to experience. I want to show my children the richness of the world more than anything. I crave new experiences like a toddler who just learned to walk. And, to travel in style with kids requires money, and quite a bit of it.

Our consumer society wants us to spend what we earn. Marketing messages bombard us from the time we wake up to the time we go to sleep. If you have a dollar, you're supposed to spend it (and save for your children's education at the same time). Credit has become so obscenely easy to obtain that we often spend money before we have it. But if you want to achieve financial independence, you will need to spend less money than you earn. I know this may not sound sexy. But when you start looking at how achievable it can actually be, you may start to get excited.

No one ever got wealthy spending more than they earn.

Warren Buffett views every dollar spent not just as a dollar spent today, but rather in terms of its potential value *after* investing and compounding over time. So how much is that cute pair of boots really costing you? When you think like this, all of a sudden, splurging seems a lot less tempting. I once read that Buffett ate an inexpensive breakfast every day even though he could afford a much more elaborate meal.

Search on the term "FIRE" (an acronym for Financial Independence Retire Early) and you will discover blog posts and podcasts by people who have achieved financial independence in 10 years or less. They did it by living frugally, saving, and investing a large portion of their income. A man who goes by the moniker of Mr. Money Mustache started this movement. He and his wife retired by the age of 30 – when their passive income met their living expenses – and raised their son without needing to work! The FIRE community believes that people enjoy working when they are able to choose what to work on. FIRE retirees work because they want to work. Mr. Money Mustache, for example, is a carpenter. He builds properties for fun. He bought a ramshackle place in his community, renovated it and rents it out to other entrepreneurs as a co-working space at super affordable prices because he does not need to make a big profit.

Now, take a moment to take your financial pulse. Where are you right now in terms of savings, debt, and investments? Where do you want to be? What are your goals? What are your stretch goals? When do you want to retire? Do you want to put yourself or your kids through school? Write down your goals. Make them SMART: Specific, Measurable, Achievable, Relevant and Time-Bound.

How far away is your reality from your goals? One reason for this book is to help you close the gap.

I discovered the power of written goals when I decided I wanted to buy a house. We had a 3-year-old and a baby in a 2-bedroom apartment. We were bursting at the seams, and every time I wrote a rent check, I cringed. I knew I was paying down our landlord's mortgage, and I wasn't building anything tangible in return. Real estate in the Greater Boston area, where I live, is very expensive.

I crunched the numbers and figured that I needed to make $250,000 in gross commissions in one year as a real estate agent in order to have the money for a down-payment on a new home and also pay off some debts. I wrote down a specific, time-bound goal, and I backed it up with a super-strong motivation. As we neared year-end, I tallied up my total earnings and realized that I was within $1,000 of my goal. My mind was blown, and I have written down my goals every year since!

I like to break goals down into 1-year, 5-year, 10-year and 20-year milestones. Gary Keller, the CEO of Keller Williams Realty, says we often overestimate what we can do in one year, but we underestimate what we can do in 5 years. Practice thinking big and set your sights high. Try doubling your initial goal. Why? Because the plan you will need to create to make the higher goal a reality will force you to change your behavior. On the other hand, small goals will let you keep doing the same things. And nothing happens without some kind of behavior change. As you've no doubt heard, if you keep doing the same thing, you will keep getting the same results. You need to think big.

- My 5-year goal is financial independence, i.e., my passive income will at least equal my expenses.
- In 10 years, I will have the ability to fund my children's college education = $300k in bank and able to pay out $100k / year for 8 years after that.

- In 20 years, I will give $1MM away to charity. That's when I will know I am truly wealthy.

Put some thought into your goals for yourself and your family if applicable. Write them down or print them out. Date and sign the paper. This is your contract with yourself. Share them with your family and friends. (If they don't laugh at you, your goals are not big enough!) The universe will conspire to bring your goals to fruition.

Call it the Secret, the Law of Attraction, or God helps those who help themselves...once you have made the desire of your heart known to the universe, the universe will help you attain it. You don't have to know the How right now. Just take action. Any action. Brainstorm a list of actions you could take to move yourself closer to your goal. Talk to people who have done it before. Read books. Take a class. Attend a networking event or seminar. Get an accountability partner. Get to work. As you take steps toward your goal, new possibilities and opportunities will arise that you haven't even thought of yet. Work earnestly toward your goal and stay open to these opportunities. They may come in a form that you don't recognize at first. Just the act of working toward your goal can change your life even before you reach the goal.

3

WHY INVEST?

*My poor dad always said,
"Work hard and save money."
My rich dad always said, "If you
want to be wealthy and financially
secure, working hard and saving
money will not get you there."*

—*Robert Kiyosaki, "Rich Dad, Poor Dad"*

Why should you invest? In a word, inflation. A dollar is not worth what it was a few decades, or even a few years, ago. The value of money continues to decline over time. If you are simply saving, your money is steadily falling behind inflation. (Unless you are saving in a high interest savings account; in that case, you may have a slight edge over the rate of inflation.) However, if you have the same money invested, your money will grow over time from compounding interest and appreciation. If you are not investing, you are actually losing money. Warren Buffett spends money frugally because he knows that when he invests a dollar, it grows exponentially. Therefore, by spending a dollar now, he is actually losing $10 or $20 in the future if he had he invested it.

In *Rich Dad Poor Dad*, Robert Kyosaki explains that when you invest, your money works for you, rather than having to work for your money. Companies no longer routinely offer pensions. At the same time, people are living longer. If we retire when we are 65, we may live another 30 years. That's a long time. We are expected to save for retirement. However, saving alone usually won't allow us to live a comfortable retirement after accounting for inflation. Furthermore, investing can yield passive income, or income that you don't have to work for. In other words, you can be making money while you sleep. An investor with passive income can relax on a beach somewhere while still getting paid because their money works for them, instead of the other way around. Investment dividends, book royalties, company revenue and rental income are all forms of passive income. If you are young, 65 may feel like an eternity away. And yet, that's exactly why you should start now. The sooner you invest, the sooner the compounding effect will get to work for you.

The graph below from *Business Insider* illustrates how starting early such as at age 25 (top line) will accumulate double the amount compared to someone starting at age 35 (bottom line). However, you can start at 40 with double the savings rate and still do quite well (middle line). The message – start early and save as much as you can.

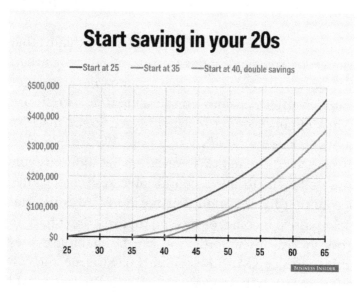

Figure 3. The Advantages of Saving

I highly recommend listening to the Bigger Pockets podcast on Financial Independence. The hosts interview people who have achieved FI, and they share their biggest financial mistakes as well as their secrets to success. Their stories will motivate you to keep on track so you can reach your financial goals.

4

WHAT'S YOUR BIG WHY?

*"Your future is whatever you make it,
so make it a good one!"*

—*Doc Brown, "Back to the Future"*

Your Big Why is the fuel to your financial plan. Working your plan will require passion, dedication and consistent effort. When you have a Big Why that inspires you, working your plan will feel like a passion project. Have you ever read a book that you just couldn't put down? That's how you will feel about your Big Why once you identify it. You will be obsessed in a good way – energized and constantly finding new avenues to bring you closer to it. It is worth taking some time to meditate on it. Often your Big Why is hidden at first.

Money is energy that allows us to buy goods, services and experiences to survive. Money represents freedom to do and have what we want. It only makes sense to want plenty of it. Some people like to spend money on shoes, some love to travel, some want a beautiful home, some just want the security of having a stockpile of money in the bank. Others want to give it away or leave a legacy to their kids. (I want all of those things!) Whatever your heart's desire, it is legitimate, no matter how seemingly frivolous. It's your life. What makes you happy? What does money mean to you? Does it mean luxury? Security? Freedom? Ability to give to others? When you attach meaning to your financial goals, they start to have emotional weight and you will become much more passionate in striving to reach them.

ACTION STEP: Stop right now and make a list of the <u>10 things or experiences that make you most happy</u>.

1.

2.

3.

4.

5.

6.

7.

8.

9.

10.

Does your actual spending align with your happiness list? Are you spending money on expensive clothes to keep up with your friends or because it makes you happy? *Uncouple happiness from spending.* The key to happiness is not wanting more than you have.

I moved a lot as a child and grew to crave stability and security in my adult life. After we had our second child, I became determined to buy a house. Moreover, my husband and I decided to buy a 2-family home to have rental income offset our mortgage. I knew this would be the foundation of our family's financial security. I wanted a house so badly for the space we desperately needed and for security for our growing family. When I calculated my earnings at the end of the year and realized I had hit my goal almost to the dollar, I truly understood the importance of having a specific goal <u>and</u> a Big Why behind it. Although the house purchase was a short-term goal for me, it aligned with my bigger goal of financial security for my family. A desire for financial security later evolved into a passion for helping others achieve financial security and independence. This gets me out of bed every morning – sometimes at 4 am – because I am so passionate about it.

What is your Big Why? If this is the first time you have thought about it, it will probably take a little while to figure it out. It is already there inside you although perhaps subconsciously. When you consciously define it, it ignites your passion and powers you forward.

ACTION STEP: Take a couple sheets of paper from a notebook or journal and set a timer for 10 minutes. Start writing about your Big Why in a stream of consciousness. There is no right or wrong. Just write everything that pops into your head, as much as you can. Don't edit or omit anything. Then, put it away.

Go back in one week and review what you wrote. Look for themes. Maybe something will jump out at you, and you might have an A-ha moment. Maybe as you ruminate on it, the ultimate goal or desire will slowly come into focus. When you discover your Big Why, it might feel familiar because your subconscious has known it all along and has already been working toward it. When you bring it out into your conscious mind, however, you can now take a targeted aim instead of being pulled along by an invisible force in the dark. You will have a much better chance of getting there sooner.

Go one more level. Visualize yourself reaching your goal.

- How does it make you feel?
- What is important to you about that feeling?
- Why is it important to you?
- Ultimately, what will all of that do for you?

Think about how you will feel when you reach your goal. What is that feeling you are striving for?

When I really thought about it, I discovered that underlying my goal of financial independence is ultimately a desire to be my best self. With all the gifts given to me, I felt a deep responsibility to be the best version of myself. Then I thought: Hold on a tic, I can be my best possible self *right now*. I don't really have to wait for my bank account to reach a certain number. In fact, when I am my best self every day, I will more easily attract financial independence to me. So, who do you have to *be* to obtain your goal?

5

WHAT IS NET WORTH AND WHY SHOULD YOU CARE?

*"If you are born poor it's not your mistake,
but if you die poor, it's your mistake."*

—Bill Gates

Net worth is simply the value of your assets minus the value of your liabilities.

Assets are things that put money in your pocket, such as cash-flowing properties, an ownership stake in a profitable business, a book residual or a profit share tree, such as at Keller Williams. Liabilities are things that take money away from you, such as debts or mooching uncles. As Ben Kinney, a mega-agent at Keller Williams says, net worth is simply a reflection of your financial decisions over time.

Make two columns, one for your assets (things you own such as cash, investments, equity in your house or car) and one for your liabilities (debts such as home and auto loans, credit card balances). If you own property, write the estimated current market value(s) in the assets column. Write the amount of the mortgage(s) in the liabilities column. Add up to the two columns and compare the figures. The difference represents your equity. Also, in the assets column, write down the balance of all your bank accounts, investment accounts, and any other valuables you own. In the liabilities column, write down any other debts you have including credit cards, student loans, personal loans and any back taxes. Add up both columns and deduct your total liabilities from your total assets. The result is your net worth.

Track your net worth over time. Make it a game with yourself to continually increase it by paying down debts if applicable and accumulating more assets. Remember Life and Monopoly, the board games you played growing up? Your calculation of net worth is your real life scorecard. Play to win! Robert Kiyosaki created a game called *Cashflow* that clearly demonstrates the power of building net worth and passive income to get out of the rat race. It's a step up from Monopoly and is great practice for an asset-building mindset. Gather some of your friends together who are also interested in building wealth and play!

Mindset is almost everything. Like Henry Ford said, "Whether you think you can or you think you can't, you're right." Your beliefs determine your actions, reactions and your results. *You can only achieve as much as you believe you are capable of and deserve.* Can you see yourself achieving your goals? Will you flourish to your highest potential? Visualization puts you there in your imagination, and your imagination is a powerful force. There is a plethora of books about improving your mindset. Acknowledge the importance of your mindset and continuously train your mind and feed it positive messages. Read *"The Secret," "Think and Grow Rich"* and *"Miracle Morning"* to get started. Daily practice of any combination of reading, affirmations, visualizations and meditation will yield powerful results. Physical exercise works wonders for mindset. One of my favorite affirmations is: "I am a money magnet." It makes me smile and helps me feel abundant. As a reminder, I custom ordered a money-shaped magnet on my fridge with my face in place of Ben Franklin's.

Figure 4. Carey's Money Magnet

I give these to the agents whom I coach to remind them they too are money magnets. If you want a money magnet for your fridge, just let me know and I'll send you one!

I recently taught a class called *Quantum Leap for Young Adults (QL)*, created by Gary Keller. Gary says that we can achieve anything we want in five years. He encourages us to think big. For example, when Gary started Keller Williams back in the 80's in Austin, TX, he set out to build the #1 brokerage in the U.S. In 2018, KW became the #1 brokerage in the *world* by number of agents, number of listings sold and sales volume. And he has changed a great many number of lives in the process. What would have happened if he had set his sights small? His goal might have been to become the #1 brokerage in Austin, or the #1 brokerage in Texas. Sure, these are worthy goals. Yet, if he had limited his vision to that scale, he probably wouldn't have developed the systems and infrastructure that allowed his company to grow so much bigger. We all have infinite potential. Yet we choose to limit ourselves.

In *The 4-Hour Workweek*, Tim Ferriss suggests that bigger goals are actually easier to achieve than mediocre goals. Why is that? Because the vast majority of people aim for mediocre goals, not believing that they can be great or do great things. If you have big goals, you will have less competition. Get out of the fray. Aim high.

I say mindset is *almost* everything because you also have to take action to see results. Right mindset coupled with right action leads to right results. When you see results, you become more confident, which leads to more results!

6

OK, SO YOU ARE GOING TO INVEST! WHAT ARE YOUR OPTIONS?

"Compound interest is the eighth wonder of the world. He who understands it, earns it ... he who doesn't ... pays it. Compound interest is the most powerful force in the universe."

– Albert Einstein

Now that we know we want—wait, scratch that—*need* to invest, let's look at the various vehicles available to us for putting our money to work for us.

The important factors to weigh when analyzing each investing tool are the following:

- return on investment (ROI)
- risk

- up-front capital needed
- expertise required to invest.

Ideally, we want the best return on investment with the least risk and with minimal up-front costs and expertise required. Please note, I am not a financial planner or an expert on stocks. This overview is only intended to give a broader context to a discussion on real estate investing. Please consult a financial expert for more details. With that said, here is my very general overview of investment vehicles.

- Savings Account: This is no longer considered an investment vehicle because the low rates of return offered by most banks doesn't even keep pace with inflation. It is slightly better than stuffing your cash under your mattress, but not by much. The best use of your savings account is to save for short-term goals such as buying a car, going on vacation, or a rainy-day fund. Some institutions offer high-yield savings accounts. If you are planning to hold a substantial amount of money in a savings account for any length of time, look into a high-yield savings account. This is about as low risk as you can get and will give you a slight edge over inflation.
- Stock Market: Probably the most well-known vehicle for investing, the stock market can be utilized by anyone and in various ways. An

individual investor can pick and choose their own individual stocks, invest in mutual funds (collections of stocks compiled by a fund manager), contribute to an IRA or a 401k (which will in turn be invested by the account holder into the stock market and dividends passed through to the investor), or the individual can hire a Financial Advisor to manage their portfolio for them. Mutual funds are a popular option because, by nature, they are diversified. Your money will be spread out among the stocks chosen by the fund manager, decreasing your risk should any one stock's value go down. In general, mutual funds are a relatively low risk, moderate return option.

- IRA's and 401k's are popular retirement investment accounts due to their tax advantages. With a traditional IRA, you invest money before it is taxed. You do have to pay taxes on it when you withdraw from it later. However, because you are compounding interest for the life of the IRA on a greater initial investment than it would have been after-tax, your money grows faster. With a Roth IRA, you invest after-tax dollars, and you do not have to pay tax when you withdraw. If you expect to be in a higher tax bracket when you withdraw – after age 59 ½ and 5 years after opening the account – the Roth IRA may be the best option. The Roth also allows you more flexibility to make some qualified early with-drawals such as a first-time home purchase, post-secondary education expenses and health insurance premiums while unemployed. There is also a self-employed IRA program (SEP) that allows a self-employed person to make greater tax-deductible contributions annually - $55,000 instead of $5,500 as of 2018 – which can really help with the tax hit. Check with your CPA about the best option for you.

IRA's and 401K's are excellent foundations for your investment portfolio. They are relatively safe, easy to set up and with only a minimal investment, $500 or $50 with a $50/month automatic contribution, for example. An automatic contribution is a great idea so you don't have to think about it and the money will continue to flow into the account without your even noticing it. We are all incredibly busy, so set it and forget it is the way to go. Your account manager, Fidelity or Schwab, for example, will allocate the assets among a variety of stocks and bonds and show you the growth on at least a quarterly basis. There are a bunch of investing apps available now such as Acorns and Albert that allow you to easily and automatically transfer funds from your bank account into an investment account right from your phone. However, it is usually equally as easy to withdraw money from those accounts. The good thing about IRA's and 401k's is that you will face penalties for early withdrawals (except for qualified events as mentioned above), so you will be much more incentivized to leave the money there for your retirement.

Generally, the stock market increases over time at a rate of about 6-11%, which is not bad, especially when compounded over many years. Don't wait to get started investing. The younger you are, the more time you have on your side for that compounding interest to work for you. I just had this conversation with my nine-year-old son. If he starts investing his extra money now, his money will be working for him by the time he's my age!

Whereas stocks are ownership stakes, bonds are loans. When an entity issues a bond, it is accepting a loan with the agreement to pay interest for the use of the money. Stocks are simply shares of individual companies. Bonds have a set duration and a set interest rate based on the level of risk investors incur. While stocks are volatile (they can go up and down), bonds are stable, the biggest risks being the issuer going bankrupt or inflation increasing to wipe out dividends. Furthermore, when stocks go up, bonds tend to go down, so it makes sense for most investors to invest in both stocks and bonds, and most mutual funds consist of a combination of both. You can buy a government bond directly from the U.S. Treasury at TreasuryDirect.gov. They are low risk and low yield, and there are no commissions or transaction costs to purchase them this way. You can also buy corporate bonds where the dividends increase as the stability of the issuer decreases, or you can buy a bond mutual fund.

Fund Rise is one example of crowd-funded real estate investing with a minimum of $500 initial investment diversified across 48+ real estate projects ranging from 9-15% returns. This is a form of passive real estate investment and is somewhat similar to the stock market in terms of risk and rewards.

As good as the above-mentioned investment products are, they are passive or "packaged investing." The benefit is they require very little to no expertise or effort. Anyone with $50 can call Fidelity or USAA and set up an IRA. With a little financial education, however, you can become a "Professional Investor" and have more control over your money to realize greater returns. Of course, this comes with greater risk as well. However, gaining financial literacy will help you minimize your risk.

So, what are the other investment options? Ready to get your hands dirty? You could invest in a business – either your own or someone else's. There are too many variables with this option to cover here. You would have to do a lot of research on the business you decide to start or invest in and be fully informed before going in. Many start-up's fail. In fact, statistics show that most businesses don't last beyond 5 years. If you pick a winner, however, you could realize tremendous returns. I'm sure you know that there are plenty of tech millionaires and billionaires who happen to have been with a company that skyrocketed in growth.

There is a digital, low-risk option for investing in businesses as well. I have come across one called Yield Street, and there are probably others.

This brings us to real estate. One significant difference from stocks is that real estate has inherent value. Whereas the value of a stock can go to zero (think Great Depression or the dot com bust), a piece of real estate always has value because it has the ability to be a home. Land is one thing they're not making any more of! Whether land or a building on land, a piece of real estate always has *some* inherent value.

Owning real estate also offers you more control than owning shares or lending money to someone else's company. Real estate values increase over time historically, so you benefit from appreciation on an average of 3-5% per year. Of course, your best bet is to hold real estate more than five years because the market can decrease in the short term. Appreciation, however, is not the primary reason real estate is an excellent asset. In fact, it's not necessarily an asset unless it produces income. According to Robert Kiyosake, your primary residence is not an asset – unless it puts money in your pocket every month. Therefore, if you live in a multi-family home and the rents flowing from the other units cover your expenses and produce a positive cash flow, your home (or the property as a whole) is indeed an asset. Otherwise, if you pay out each month for your home, then it is considered a liability because it takes money away from you even though you are building equity.

7

WHY REAL ESTATE?

*"I will forever believe that buying a home
is a great investment. Why? Because you
can't live in a stock certificate. You can't
live in a mutual fund."*

—*Oprah Winfrey*

According to a recent study by the Federal Reserve, the 2016 median net worth of renters was $5,200 (bottom line in the figure below) and at the same time, the median net worth of homeowners was $231,400, or 44 times that of renters (top line). (Source: Keeping Current Matters, Oct. 12, 2017.) So even though your home is usually not an asset per se, the equity in it contributes to your net worth. Paying down a mortgage could be viewed as forced savings. Every mortgage payment pays down some of the principal of the loan and increases the owner's equity in the property. This is a great benefit to owning your home rather than renting. When you are renting, you are still paying for housing every month, yet you will never see that money again.

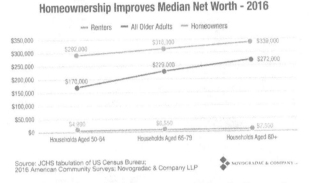

Figure 5. Improvement in Net Worth through Homeownership

I recently read *"I Will Teach You to Be Rich"* by Ramit Sethi. If you haven't read it, I recommend it. It's a practical, no-nonsense approach to personal finance tailored to Millennials. I love that Ramit strongly encourages us to automate finances because people are inherently lazy, and we can use this to our advantage by setting up automatic bill pay and savings. Once you have the system set up, you only need to look at it once a month to check that everything is going as planned. He says money should not be exciting or dramatic; it should be boring because after you make the plan, you simply follow the plan and let time do the

Benefits of Investing in Residential Real Estate Properties

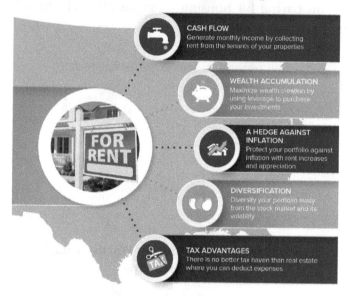

CASH FLOW
Generate monthly income by collecting rent from the tenants of your properties

WEALTH ACCUMULATION
Maximize wealth creation by using leverage to purchase your investments

A HEDGE AGAINST INFLATION
Protect your portfolio against inflation with rent increases and appreciation

DIVERSIFICATION
Diversify your portfolio away from the stock market and its volatility

TAX ADVANTAGES
There is no better tax haven than real estate where you can deduct expenses

**Figure 6. Benefits of Investing in Real Estate.
Source: HomeUnion.com**

work for you. He also motivates us to get started investing today because every second we wait costs us money down the road. However, when it comes to real estate, we have a difference of opinion.

I was enjoying the book and appreciating his sound, common-sense advice until I got to the part about real estate. He argues that real estate is not a good investment because you will just roll the equity you gain into another property when you sell. Seriously? That may be true for your primary residence. However, when you are renting, you have absolutely nothing to show for all those payments you have made when you move on to your next home. Also, your rent will almost definitely increase over time while your fixed mortgage payment will stay the same. And at some point, you can pay your mortgage off entirely! This will *never* happen with your rent!

Also, if you are a landlord who owns income properties, you are the recipient of the passive income from your rental properties, and again, while the rents increase over time, your mortgage payments can stay the same. When you sell your investment real estate, there is no need to purchase another property unless you want to. You may choose to save, re-invest or spend your proceeds. I definitely think you have to take caution and be educated before investing in real estate. You want to make sure you can manage the monthly payments and not just calculate in the principal and interest, but also the taxes, insurance and maintenance. You should have a cushion in case of unexpected expenses. But if you do it right, the pros of real estate investing far outweigh the cons. Maybe Sethi has never had the patience to invest in real estate, but everyone has their own opinion.

Real estate can yield exceptional returns because you can *leverage* your money using mortgages. Mortgages allow you to invest for 20 cents on the dollar (or sometimes less). While a down-payment of anywhere from 5-25% of the purchase price might still be a hefty sum, it allows you to control a property worth much more than your initial investment. Whereas, when you invest in stocks, you buy them in a 1-to-1 ratio, when you buy real estate, you are using the lender's money to cover most of the cost of the purchase. (Even if you buy stocks on margin, you still cannot control much of a multiple of your cash on hand.) Let's say you buy a $200,000 property with 20% down and the property appreciates 5% in one year, a healthy appreciation rate in a stable market. The property value increases to $210,000. You have just gained $10,000 on your initial cash investment of $40,000. Therefore, you have increased your initial investment by 25% in just one year by doing absolutely nothing except making your monthly housing payments. Recall that a good return in the stock market is 8-11%. The leveraging power of financing allows for better returns in real estate. Furthermore, you can purchase a property with as little as 3.5% down using an FHA loan. Real estate allows you to leverage OPM (Other People's Money) to yield returns.

After working as a real estate agent for a few years, I began to realize that while my seller clients netted huge profits from selling investment properties in their later years, many of my younger buyers didn't even have real estate investment on their radar. When I mentioned the possibility of buying a two-family instead of a condo in a buyer consultation, living in one unit and renting out the other, most of the time their eyes would glaze over. Unless their parents had talked to them about it or had done it themselves, my buyers weren't even considering this as a possibility. And for a long time, I wondered why. I saw it as such an amazing opportunity to build wealth and obtain financial security over a lifetime, but my peers weren't thinking the same way. Later, I came across a statistic on Homes.com where a study showed that 40% of Americans ranked buying a home as the most stressful thing in life. I realized that if people think buying a home is that stressful, buying an income property probably seems completely overwhelming.

However, if you know what you're doing and have some education, you can definitely do it. People from all walks of life have been investing in real estate for hundreds of years. Boatloads of immigrants have built fortunes after arriving in this country with only the clothes on their backs. Foreign investors are currently buying up real estate in our country like hotcakes. Most of the richest people in the world obtained their wealth through real estate. You have this opportunity all around you.

The wealth you desire is literally beneath your feet. So, don't let anyone tell you it's not a good investment. You don't have to be a genius. Just use common sense, have a great team around you, and follow some simple guidelines. I will share some ways to get into the investing market as a first-timer with very little money down and very little risk. As with all investing, there's always going to be some risk. That's life. But I'll show you how to mitigate that and make it a lot less scary. I will outline the steps to building your real estate empire. It all starts in your own backyard.

8

WHY DO PEOPLE FEAR REAL ESTATE INVESTING?

*"Owning a home is a keystone of wealth:
both financial affluence and
emotional security."*

—*Russell Sage*

Here are some of the reasons people don't invest in real estate:

- Large sums of money are involved
- Decisions often have to be made quickly involving said large sums of money
- The C word: Commitment – 30-year mortgages – Yikes!
- Maintenance – calls in the middle of the night to fix broken toilets? Double yikes!

- The Unknown – lack of education. We don't know what we don't know.
- Analysis paralysis – Many people get interested, read every book on the subject, attend every seminar, and never take action!

Obviously, you need to exercise caution when it comes to real estate investing, as with any investing (or spending for that matter). However, in my experience, the bigger problem for would-be investors tends to be TOO MUCH CAUTION, rather than too little. When people sit on the sidelines and never take action, they are in effect, LOSING MONEY. They are losing the potential gains that they could realize by starting NOW.

As the Chinese proverb says, the best time to plant a tree was 20 years ago. The second-best time is today.

Take it from my clients who are selling income properties for a profit. Their only regret is that they didn't buy more of them!

**Figure 7. Real Estate Price Appreciation.
Source: 2019 Realtor.com**

9

REAL ESTATE INVESTING STRATEGIES

"If you don't own a home, buy one. If you own a home, buy another one. If you own two homes, buy a third. And, lend your relatives money to buy a home."

—*John Paulson, investor and multi-billionaire*

There are several real estate investing strategies. This chapter focuses on three of the most popular and effective.

Strategy #1. The House Hack

Who doesn't love a good life hack? The house hack strategy can serve as the foundation for your financially free life by allowing you to significantly reduce life's largest expense. Conventional wisdom says to spend no more than one third of your income on housing, whether you rent or own, which makes housing our single largest expense in most cases. House-hacking allows you to offset that expense with rental income making it possible to spend much less for housing, or sometimes live for free or even have a positive cash flow. As an added benefit, you will also build up equity while someone else pays your mortgage! This is a great way to start your real estate investing career.

Ben Kinney, a Keller Williams mega-agent, started out life in absolute poverty. As a child, he lived with his divorced father in a cluttered 260-sf cabin with no plumbing or electricity. He didn't have a bed. His father broke a couch in half and each of them slept on one half. He tells the story of when he first discovered the opportunities real estate offered. He was working for a cable company at the time. On a house call, he complimented the customer's new condo. She clarified that it was not a condo; it was a duplex. He asked her what the difference was. She explained that she owned both sides of the property, and the tenant in the other unit pays her entire mortgage. Ben Kinney realized that this lady lives for free. Inspired, Kinney went home, called a mortgage broker and found out he would need $11,500 for a down-payment to buy a duplex in his area. He put his head down and worked overtime until he accumulated $11,500 in savings. He then went out and bought a duplex, got a tenant, and the rental income paid the entire mortgage less $10 a month. This was his first foray into real estate.

Ben is now a superstar agent, business owner, investor and millionaire. I saw him give a presentation once called *Give a Million* where he taught how to make enough money to be able to give away $1MM to charity. He's come a long way from that shack in the woods! He emphasizes that he is *not a genius*. He believes that if he can do it, you can too.

Some people house-hack with a condo or single family too, by renting out rooms to friends. It could even be done while renting by sub-leasing extra rooms. House-hacking reduces your housing expense and allows you to save or invest that income instead, speeding up your journey to financial independence.

Figure 8. Typical Two-Family Home

This is a photo of a lovely 2-family home that our client, Wendy, a nurse, bought a few years ago. She lives in one unit and rents out the other. She followed in her parents' footsteps who did the same thing when they were her age. Her tenant's rent offsets a large portion of her housing costs, so every month, she builds equity while saving money on her living expenses.

Before we purchased our two-family home, we rented a small, 2-bedroom apartment for $1600/month. We purchased the 2-family for $500,000 with 10% down. We live in one unit, and our rental unit brings in $1800/month. The mortgage plus taxes is $2800/ month. Less the rental income, our portion of the monthly payment is about $1000. We pay approximately $5000/year or $416/month for water and insurance. Therefore, we spend less per month to own a large 2-family home than did for that little apartment. And, after we moved out, our old landlord has increased the rent for that apartment to $2200. Meanwhile, the market rent for our rental unit continues to climb every couple of years and further closes the gap between our housing expenses and rental income.

The relationship between cost of ownership and renting will depend on the market you live in. Some markets will support house-hacking more than others.

For example, just a few years ago, Eric, a young entrepreneur, purchased a three-family home in Portland, Maine, as a first-time homebuyer with only 3% down. He lives in one unit and rents out the other two. He refinanced 2 years later and was able to drop PMI (Private Mortgage Insurance) and raised the rents to market value. The rents from the other two units now cover both the mortgage and property expenses, *and* there is some left over. He not only lives for free, but his home produces a positive cash-flow to boot. Not bad for 28 years old! He was fortunate to have help from his parents with the down-payment, which he later repaid. If your parents are able and willing to do this for you, be very grateful! If not, though, don't let it stop you! Find out how much you need and find a way to get there.

The most common challenge in real estate investing is coming up with the down-payment. However, if you live in the property, it qualifies as your primary residence making you eligible for a lower down-payment such as 3, 5 or 10% of the purchase price. This makes breaking into the market a lot more accessible than if you had to save up 20 or 25%, when you do not live in the property. Take advantage of this opportunity to make your home an investment. Talk to a preferred lender in your market about which programs are available to you.

What you buy depends on your situation, how much you save, and the goal you have in mind. First, identify the goal – how much money do you realistically need to put down on a property, cover closing costs and have a cushion for maintenance? How long will it take you to reach your goal? Challenge yourself to save as much of your income as possible in order to reach your goal as soon as possible. Can you save 10% of your income? How about 30 or 40%? Get creative.

The FIRE movement eschews American consumerism in favor of a hyper-focused attention on budgeting, saving and investing in order to obtain financial freedom at an early age. They have found creative ways of whittling down their recurring expenses and living well below their means. By house-hacking, biking or ride-sharing instead of owning a car, for example, they reduce their monthly expenditures to 50% or even 40% of their income, and they invest the rest. After just ten years of extreme budgeting and conservative investing, they are able to retire and live off the dividends of their investments.

If you abhor budgeting, I get it. I love spending money, and I value spontaneity and freedom. I enjoy having the freedom to spend when I want to. However, when I started hearing these amazing stories of people reclaiming their time and having the ability to do only what makes them happy, my perspective on budgeting changed. Now, if I choose not to buy something, it's not because I can't afford it; it's because I choose to work towards financial freedom instead. Spending frivolously is not freedom. Having enough passive income to live while not having to work is real freedom. And, deep down, I know that we don't really need most of the stuff we fill our lives with anyway. Take an inventory of what you are actually spending money on. How many recurring subscriptions do you have? What do they all amount to in a year? What do you spend on going out every month? In a year? How much could you save if you cooked at home? It may seem tedious at first, but try making it a game. How little could you spend? How much could you save? The minute you start seeing how your money can work for you while you sleep, budgeting becomes a lot more fun!

Strategy #2. The Owner-Occupant Flip

You don't have to be a developer or an HGTV host to flip a house. As in the house-hack strategy, you can take advantage of the lower down-payment loan programs offered to owner-occupants to use your primary residence as an investment vehicle. As an owner-occupant, you can also get a tax exemption on the gains as long as you hold the property for more than two years (up to $250k for an individual and $500k as a married couple as of 2018). Because tax laws can change, check with your CPA on anything tax-related.

Buy smart: find a property that needs some work and add value to it while you're living there. Buddy up with a reputable contractor who gives free quotes to help you calculate the expenses of improvements.

Our first home purchase was a foreclosed condo in Los Angeles. We had an inspection, and the structure and systems were solid, yet it needed cosmetics such as paint, new light fixtures, and small things like a towel rack in the bathroom, new window treatments, etc.

Also, it was a one-bedroom condo with a loft, and we saw an opportunity to add a wall and create a second bedroom. We hired someone to add the wall and hired a painter for one of the rooms because it had vaulted ceilings. My husband refinished the deck, we did more painting ourselves and added some touches throughout. It was so satisfying to see the before and after!

Our renovations cost less than $10k, and we sold for over $50k more than we bought for just one year later, even though it was a down market. We were not intending to flip the property when we bought it, mind you. We had a change of plans and chose to sell one year later because we decided to move closer to our families after our son was born. If we had stayed longer as we had initally planned, our returns would have increased. Also, because we flipped it in less than two years, we had to pay taxes on the profit. Due to our life circumstances and our priorities at the time, our returns were fairly modest. However, the profit we made still helped us make our cross country move and change careers.

Flipping means adding value to a property over and above the expense invested into it. You are making $1 + 1 = 3$. Our LA flip opened my eyes to a whole new world where you can make money by *adding value* instead of by trading time for a paycheck. The returns can far outweigh the time you spend, so the potential opportunity is almost limitless. Let's look at some examples using a metric called Return on Investment. Here is a simple formula:

Return on Investment = ROI = (Gain from Investment - Cost of Investment) / Cost of Investment, expressed as a percentage or ratio. (Investopedia.com)

Some clients of mine bought a foreclosed condo as their first home for $145,000. They put down 5% as a down payment. They made cosmetic improvements, spending about $20k. Including closing costs, their initial investment was about $30k. I sold it for them three years later for $270,000. After costs of sale, the net proceeds from the sale was $89,000. After subtracting the initial investment of $30k, their gain was $59k. Their ROI was roughly 200%. In other words, they *doubled* their initial investment in 3 years. Because they lived there for more than 2 years, they did not have to pay capital gains tax. For comparison, as a yearly ROI, this is about 66% per year. Whereas, 8% would be an excellent return in the stock market. Because they leveraged their money by financing 95% of the purchase price, their return on their investment was through the roof because they made a killer profit. They bought smart and reaped the benefits.

Some other clients bought an off-market condo that needed some work. It was a For Sale By Owner. They bought the condo for $340k with $50,000 down. Three years later, after making approximately $30k of improvements, they sold the condo for $525,000. Their net profit was about $155,000 making their total ROI over the 3 year period roughly 200% or 66% per year.

As you can see, flipping can yield powerful results when done right.

Some people choose to flip their primary residence two, three or four times in a row, moving from one property to the next and building up more equity every time. You have to decide how much you like moving and renovating a home while living there. For me, once was enough, since we had a baby. If I had been turned onto real estate investing sooner, I may have done it a couple more times before having kids. The great returns help to mitigate the inconvenience of living in a construction zone.

Ideally, you will want to find something that just needs minor repairs and cosmetic updates since these are less costly and less intrusive than major renovations. In addition, they usually come with fewer surprises.

You can also combine strategies #1 and #2. When we bought our two-family home, we found one that needed some work. We had the work pretty much finished before we moved in. I always advise buying a property that has potential for sweat equity. This doesn't mean you have to do the work yourself! Hire an excellent contractor and ask your Realtor to help you decide which improvements will give you the most bang for your buck. Seek out a property that has "good bones" – in other words, it is structurally and mechanically sound – that just needs some cosmetic updating. Look for something that you can update: bathrooms, kitchens, remove wallpaper, paint, remove carpet, refinish floors, etc. In general, all these things are relatively easy and cheap to do and will add more value than you will spend. Most people already know this and yet when they are looking at houses and see one that needs work, they often get turned off. It just feels like too much work and it's hard to see past old, outdated finishes. Develop your vision and learn to see the potential.

Realtors and developers know that Millennials want move-in ready homes, are not handy and don't want to lift a finger to do anything to their house. Therefore, they are rehabbing these diamonds in the rough and selling you million-dollar condos while making hundreds of thousands of dollars! *I want you to claim that equity*! It's OK if you are not handy. That's what contractors are for. Also, this stuff is really fun! You get to play designer! Who doesn't love seeing a room or an entire house transformed by a fresh paint job and some new cabinets and light fixtures? Once you get started, you may never want to stop.

It's amazing how small touches add up to a big impact in a space. Homes evoke emotional reactions in us, so you will find that improving your space makes you feel different when you are in it. It's a way of expressing yourself. If you don't have a creative bone in your body, bring in an interior designer or stylish friend to help you with your vision. You will still benefit from the added enjoyment of and equity in your home!

The key to a good flip is to buy right. While you may be tempted to buy in the least expensive neighborhoods, the more desirable, aka expensive, the neighborhood, the greater the profit margin in a flip. You have no doubt heard the phrase, Location, Location, Location. Buy the ugliest house in the nicest neighborhood you can afford. Use finishes that are equivalent to the nicer homes in that neighborhood and you will get more bang for the cost of the renovations due to the greater desirability of the location.

Notice that in the examples above, my clients and I purchased foreclosed and off-market properties. This helped us buy below market value so that we had instant equity in the property. We will talk more about this later.

Strategy #3. BRRRR

No, I'm not chilly. This acronym stands for Buy, Rehab, Rent, Refinance, Repeat. After you have built up some capital by flipping and/or purchasing your first income property as an owner-occupant, consider buying investment properties that you do not live in. The bad news: you have to put more money down because you will not live in the property. Whereas with a primary residence you can put as little as 3.5% down, you are going to need 25% down for a pure investment property. The good news: you can Refinance your primary residence or pull a home equity line of credit to get cash for the down payment once you have enough equity. You might think this sounds risky, but what do you think the bank does with your money? They invest it and use it to get more money! You can do the same, as long as the numbers work. It is your equity, and you can leverage it to create more money. Start small. For example, invest in a condo in an up-and-coming area. I once had a client who invested in a couple of parking spaces in Boston and did very well.

Rehab the investment property to create some sweat equity, then hold it for a few years while the tenant pays down the mortgage and your equity increases. Then you Repeat the process - Refinance that property to buy another.

While flipping your own home realizes short-term gains, the BRRRR investment strategy allows you to keep your properties long-term while leveraging the equity you have created with your renovations to buy more properties. Essentially, you are combining the benefits of the House-hack (passive income) and the Flip (adding value) for a real estate investment 1-2 punch, and all while using mostly Other People's Money (OPM).

Holding rental properties long-term ideally has the *triple benefit* of cash flow, equity pay-down, and appreciation. In other words, your rental income should exceed your expenses so cash flows in your direction every month, the tenants are paying down your principal AND you are building equity every month. The property value naturally appreciates over the years, also increasing your equity. Holding investment properties long-term, and specifically using the BRRRR method, is the best way to build wealth in real estate.

Once again, that initial down payment represents the single biggest hurdle to getting this strategy off the ground. You can start by refinancing your own home.

You could also partner up and spread out the larger down payment to make it more manageable. A mega-real estate agent and investor Wendy Papasan, started out by offering to find and manage properties while her partner invested the capital. Here's the biggest secret in real estate investing: *finding money to invest is not hard!* There are wealthy people everywhere looking to invest their money for a good return. Finding the deal is harder.

How do you find partners? Talk to people. Go to networking events, seminars and meet-up's for investors. Do not be tempted by real estate investing or house-flipping mentor programs that want you to pay them thousands of dollars for the privilege of learning their tactics. You know the type – they scream at you on late-night commercials, offering free seminars and free gifts. The seminars are essentially sales pitches, and often the free gifts aren't worth more than a few dollars. It's fine to attend these seminars as networking opportunities, just don't give them your credit card info! There are so many books, online resources and networking opportunities out there on this topic for little or no money. Better yet, befriend someone who has done it before and ask them to mentor you. Seek and you will find!

Takeaways:

- Once you have built up enough equity or capital or found partners with capital, buy investment properties you don't live in.

- Your equity is your money. Why not put it to work for you?
- Rome wasn't built in a day. It takes time and patience. Get the first one under your belt and build on it.
- Start small – a single-family, condo or even a parking space.
- Partner up.

By the way, you can also enjoy certain tax benefits from owning investment property. The government gives a tax break to owners of rental real estate. This is called depreciation. It leads to a situation where a significant portion of your net profit from rental estate can be tax free. This is a fourth good reason to own rental real estate. The more you make every year, the more valuable this is.

For example, as of 2018, if you buy a property for $375,000, and the land is valued at $100,000 and you have a net profit on rental income per year of 10,000, the entire $10,000 would be untaxed! That's great, right! It is a major additional benefit of owning rental real estate. There could be other tax breaks for you.

I advise you to read up on this and to talk to your CPA so that you are up to date on IRS rules and understand how they apply to you. If you would like a referral, I am glad to give you the name of an exceptional CPA in your area.

10

WHAT KIND OF INVESTMENT PROPERTY SHOULD I BUY?

"Make your money on the buy, not the sell;
this is true in any investment whether it's
real estate, business or the stock market."

—*Ziad K. Abdelnour*

As much as I endorse real estate investing, I also endorse selectivity when it comes to making a purchase. Look at lots of properties before you actually buy one! I would rather have you say no to a good deal than say yes to a bad one because another deal will always come along.

Let's get into the nitty-gritty of the different types of properties you can buy and the pros and cons of each one. Keep in mind that markets vary greatly, so while this is a general overview, you will want to work with a trusted real estate agent and become familiar with your own market dynamics. What could be a great deal in one state, county, town, or even neighborhood could be a terrible one in another.

Residential rental properties are often the best properties you can invest in. Why? Everyone needs a home! Therefore, you can always find a tenant for your rental property as long as you are located in a desirable area and priced in line with the local rental market. Typically, they are less complicated than commercial investments as well.

Within this category, there are various types of properties you can own, each with pros and cons. Local market dynamics will factor into the investment potential of these options, so again, always partner with a top agent in your market.

1. Condos: one good thing about condos is they can be relatively cheap. You are basically buying a portion of a building instead of the whole thing, so you may be able to get into the market sooner, with less money down. Also, in some cases, you may have a higher quality tenant pool than in the multi-family rental market. However, there are also some cons to condos as rental properties. For one, there are condo fees. You have to pay them every month, and they can be unpredictable over time. So, the rent should offset those, as well as any other expenses. On the other hand, those fees typically cover shared

expenses such as water, sewer and exterior maintenance. You would also have those kinds of costs as a single- or multi-family owner, just not shared by an association.

Secondly, you do not have complete control over the property because you belong to an association. There could be additional expenses if the association decides to levy an assessment for a major repair. Another drawback is that, as opposed to a multi-family, a condo is rented to a single tenant rather than several. In case of a vacancy, this means you would have no money coming in whatsoever. Whereas with a multi, obviously, you could have one unit vacant and other units still paying rent.

Even if condos are not your ultimate investment goal, they may be a good stepping stone to a longer-term income property. If you're going to buy a condo, try to do so in an area that's increasing in value and that is highly rentable (this goes for all investment properties naturally) and make sure that the building and association are in good shape. The vast majority of condos are move-in ready when they hit the market. However, if you look hard enough, you may be able to find one that needs improvements allowing you to earn some sweat equity.

2.   Single-family homes give you more control than condos because you own the entire structure and the land. They are usually more expensive, however, and all of the maintenance falls to you rather than being

spread out among the members of a condo association. There may be a smaller pool of renters for single-family homes rather than condos depending on where you live because single-family homes tend to command higher rents. However, single-family homes are inherently desirable. In Boston, for example, developers have gone crazy building new condominiums in the past few years, saturating the condo market, while single families are not as plentiful and are therefore in high demand. Again, location is paramount. Choose a neighborhood that will attract good tenants, such as a family friendly neighborhood on a cul-de-sac and in a good school system.

3. Multi-family homes: These are nice because you have multiple units to rent out. Therefore, you can maximize your rent because the property is partitioned into two, three or more units. You have the option of living in one unit and renting out the other(s). House-hacking makes buying your first multi-family much more affordable since you can generally put down a lower down-payment. The lender will typically factor in the current rental income if there are already tenants in the building, or some portion of the potential market rent if the units are vacant when they calculate your debt-to-income ratio as they process your loan. This means you can likely afford to buy a higher priced property than you could if you were buying an owner occupant single-family.

An important note on renting residential properties: be aware of lead paint laws. In MA, any family with children under six years old has the right to demand that their landlord de-lead a home built before 1978 and contains lead paint. The landlord also has to provide alternative housing while the de-leading occurs. This could be an expensive process. So, before you buy, figure out how likely it is that there is lead paint present in the home. If it was built prior to 1978 and has not been de-leaded, chances are there is some lead paint present. Your best bet is to de-lead or buy one that's already de-leaded. If the woodwork – i.e. door frames and window frames – are *not* painted, the risk of lead paint ending up in a child's mouth is much less. If there is peeling or flaking paint anywhere, that *must* be addressed before renting. In MA, you can apply for a waiver for up to two years as long as there is no peeling or flaking paint in the home, which allows you to delay de-leading. Check with your state Board of Health for local laws. In MA, we also have fair housing laws which prevent a landlord from discriminating against families with kids, so simply choosing to turn away tenants with kids to avoid dealing with the lead paint laws is illegal. Know your rights and responsibilities to avoid liability and added expense.

If you are planning to flip a home, you may be thinking of turning a 2 or 3-family home into individual condominiums. The potential profits could be greater because you have the ability to sell to multiple buyers. However, there are a fair number of pitfalls, so I don't recommend this for your first time out unless you have an incredible opportunity. I have had clients do this for their first time and because of the various regulations the city imposes on new conversions and the sheer amount of work involved in renovating multiple units, it typically takes a LOT longer than anticipated. The condo buyer typically wants *and expects* a near-perfect product – all brand new and immaculate – so in order to compete with the other condos on the market, you will need to deliver this standard as well. One client of mine did a conversion but decided not to renovate the bathroom, for example, so it still had vintage 1950's bright pink tile and fixtures. (He did not consult me during the renovation, unfortunately.) The market responded. He did not get his asking price and had to do a major reduction in order to sell. Fortunately, he had owned the building for a very long time and had the ability to do that. If you have just purchased, you might not. Buyers will know if you cut corners.

When buying any residential rental property, consider the rental market in the area. Are you close to schools, colleges, public transportation, major employers or anything else that would consistently attract renters? The thing you really want to avoid is vacancies for any length of time. When you have a vacancy, you are still paying out holding costs for the property but not getting any income to cover the expenses. Therefore, being in a highly rentable neighborhood is key. There are hot spots in any city where a new rental listing will be snapped up the minute it comes available. If you don't know where those are, please consult an experienced, local, full-time real estate agent. Be realistic about the rental potential. When you rent at a reasonable rate, vacancies are much less likely.

My clients who have consistently kept the rents *slightly lower* than market have reported having excellent tenants who stay a long time. Tenant turnover causes a lot of wear and tear on a property, so long-term, stable tenants are worth their weight in gold. The few dollars that you forfeit in rent come back to you in spades in the form of fewer vacancies, less damage due to happy and conscientious tenants, timely rent payments, and less turnover. Tenants who feel they have a good deal naturally want to stay, so they will take good care of your property and will happily pay you on time or even early for the privilege of renting at a reasonable rate.

If you charge high rents, you may have high turnover and prolonged vacancies, both of which are costly to an owner. Besides charging fair rents, screen your tenants well. I recommend using a reputable and experienced rental agent or property manager for this. They will have a system for checking references, credit, income and employment, so that you don't have any surprises. It's worth the money for this service, as you will (hopefully) be dealing with this tenant for years to come. Price to attract multiple rental applications and be selective.

Create a spreadsheet to analyze your monthly payments and expenses for each property, making sure to factor in taxes, home insurance and any utilities you are responsible for, such as water and sewer. You should also put some money aside each month for general maintenance. You may find, as we did, that even with the expenses of ownership, that your net monthly costs are less than the rent you would pay for a similar home in the area. Think about it: the landlord you are renting from is covering their expenses and then some, otherwise they wouldn't be a landlord... so why line their pockets when you could do it for yourself? And, as time goes by, your fixed rate mortgage payments will stay the same while rents will increase. This means you can increase the rent every few years, thereby increasing your profit margin.

11

FINANCING REAL ESTATE, OR SHOW ME THE MONEY

"Money doesn't grow on trees!" – most everyone's Mom or Dad

I think that a lot of us are inadvertently trained from an early age to have a mindset of "lack" around money. It wasn't until I was in my 30's that I became aware of the messages I had unconsciously absorbed growing up and had integrated into my belief system. I have been working to undo them ever since. In so many ways, we are taught that money is bad. It is "the root of all evil." Therefore, the desire of money is greedy and wrong. As an adult, I can now see that this belief is erroneous. Money is good for the good it can do. If you are a good person and you acquire wealth, you will do good with it. If you are a bad person and you acquire wealth, you will do bad with it. However, if you have more resources to share, you are more able to be generous with them. And if you think about it, many wealthy people are naturally philanthropic. Bill and Melinda Gates are a prime example. There is only so much an individual or a family can spend on themselves. When our own needs are sated, we are inclined to give to others. This is my new belief: that when we brim with abundance, we overflow into others.

We have been told all our lives that money does not grow on trees, so it's no surprise that the #1 biggest hurdle that people face when considering investing in real estate is the initial down-payment. Saving tens of thousands of dollars can seem so overwhelming that many people never get past this thought. Additionally, because so many young people start their adult life with college debt these days and the costs of living seem to be always increasing, Millennials are especially challenged by the cost of homeownership despite their eagerness to enter the market, according to many reputable studies.

However, buying your first property could be more affordable than you think. For example, if you buy a condo that needs some TLC for $250k using an FHA loan which allows you to put 3.5% down, that would only require $8750 plus closing costs in cash. You may even be able to have the seller pay the closing costs. (For comparison, in many markets, getting into a rental requires three months up front for first, last and security, which could easily amount to $6000 or more. Before you put down money like that on a rental, look at the potential cost of buying.)

Because lending regulations and programs change a lot from year to year, it's imperative to get connected with a mortgage expert. Don't shop for rates. In my experience, *all lenders offer a comparable rate*, although some will reduce the rate and then charge more fees on the back end to make up for it. What you really want is someone who is extremely knowledgeable, responsive, trustworthy and who offers superior customer service.

Look into the Renovation Loan. This lending product allows you to finance the purchase price AND the cost of renovations on a "fixer-upper." The lender has an appraiser evaluate the property and finances the loan based on the estimated After Renovation Value (ARV). After you close on the purchase, the lender will release the renovation funds in increments as needed for the contractor to perform the work. Keep in mind, this is a more complex mortgage product and the bank will have to approve your plans and your contractor. Your contractor will also work hand-in-hand with the lender to finish each stage and have the next set of funds released. However, it's a fabulous way for investors to improve a home and add sweat equity without having to come up with another chunk of money besides the down payment.

Since the 203K renovation loan is an FHA product, you can put down as little as 3.5% of the purchase price. Credit score must be 620 or higher as of this writing. You do have to be an owner-occupant. There may be a minimum on how long you have to own before selling. Check with your mortgage broker.

As an example, using this loan you could purchase a condo for $250,000 with $9,450 down plus closing costs and hire a contractor to make $20k of cosmetic touches, such as paint, refinishing the floors, new appliances and countertops, for example. The cost of the renovation is rolled into your mortgage, so you don't have to come up with the cash. You sell it two years later for $325,000 giving you about $35k in profit after costs of selling, in addition to your initial down payment, to put down on another property.

Here are some pointers to help you get into the market as quickly as possible:

- Protect your credit like it's gold – because it is. Just a few points plus or minus on your credit score can show up as thousands of dollars in your monthly payments over the duration of the loan. It's easy to check your credit score nowadays, so keep an eye on it. Make all of your payments on time. A great way to do this is to automate your bills. Almost every payment portal offers the option of automating your monthly payments so they go through on time every month. Choose a date that is one or two days later than your paycheck so you know the funds will be there. You will save on late payment fees and preserve your credit.

- Research low down-payment options. FHA programs allow you to put as little as 3.5% down.

Some state programs could offer even lower down-payment options to first time buyers. If you are a veteran, you may qualify for a 0% down VA loan. Just watch out for PMI (private mortgage insurance). This is when the lender has you pay an additional monthly fee to insure them in case you default on the loan. If your loan requires PMI, check that you will be able to refinance to get rid of it later when you have more equity in the home. As of this writing, you can refinance an FHA loan and drop the PMI once you have 20% equity in the home.

Here is a little history lesson from american-progress.org. Prior to the introduction of the government guarantee on residential mortgages in the 1930s, mortgages typically had 50 percent down-payment requirements, short durations, and high interest rates—putting homeownership out of reach for many middle-class families. The housing finance system was subject to frequent panics during which depositors demanded cash from their banks, leaving lenders insolvent. That volatility is one reason why every other developed economy in the world has deep levels of government support for residential mortgage finance. In addition, abruptly removing government support would almost certainly mean the end of the 30-year fixed-rate mortgage, now a pillar of the U.S. housing market. For decades, middle-class families have depended on the security and affordability of this product, which allows borrowers to fix their housing costs and better plan for their futures in an ever more volatile economy. Most experts agree that this highly beneficial product would largely disappear without a government guarantee.

Have a conversation with an excellent mortgage broker well before you are ready to buy. Why? A mortgage expert can advise you on the most efficient ways to improve your credit in the time before you apply for your mortgage. They may suggest paying down a credit card or two for example. A few hundred dollars well spent could have a big impact on your score and therefore save you thousands if not tens of thousands over the life of your loan. Our mortgage broker did this for us before we bought our two-family. We had a few, small credit card balances and a car loan, and he advised us how much to pay off - to the penny - in order to raise our credit score enough to bump us up to the best possible rate.

- Private Lenders have more flexibility than conventional lenders. Typically, local banks are more likely to be "portfolio lenders" meaning they keep the loans that they make in their own portfolio rather than selling them on the secondary market, to Fannie Mae or Freddie Mac. This means that they can make common sense judgment calls regarding an individual borrower and may approve someone who could not get a preapproval through the conventional route due to tight regulations. If you are running into issues with a conventional loan, talk to a portfolio lender about their options.

- To minimize the up-front cash needed to purchase, ask the seller to cover your closing costs. The seller's concern is what she nets from the sale. As long as the net purchase price satisfies her bottom line, she won't mind if you want to roll the closing costs into the offer price.

- Maybe you have great credit but not a lot of cash. Do you have an IRA? With a traditional IRA, you can borrow up to $10k for a down payment without paying a tax penalty, although you will have to pay income tax on the loan. If you are married, each spouse can borrow up to $10k for a total of $20k. Note that these figures are as of 2018 and may change. Borrowing against your 401K may also be an option. The loan proceeds are not subject to income tax or a penalty, and the interest on the loan is paid back into the account.

- Your down payment can be a gift. If you are fortunate enough to have parents, relatives or a fairy godmother who has set money aside to help you get started, this is a great way to do it. Not only are they helping you buy a home, they are helping you make an investment with the potential to grow exponentially. You now have the opportunity to turn this gift into wealth for life. What an amazing thing for you and your parent(s) or relative. You will want to be aware of the lender's guidelines when it comes to using gifts for a down-payment. Consult your mortgage officer.

- If a parent or relative bought you whole life insurance or another type of insurance that accumulates in value over time, you may be able to borrow against your death benefit to buy a home. You can repay it later or it will be deducted from your death benefit when that time comes.

- You could partner with an investor. They provide the capital (down-payment plus any renovation costs). You find the property and manage it and, in return, send them a portion of the rental income proceeds, the sale proceeds, or both. There are limitless ways to structure a partnership. As long as it's profitable for both parties, it's all good. One thing to keep in mind here: investment capital is relatively easy to find. There are many individuals looking for a way to get a good return on their money. Finding the deal is much harder. Once you find a good real estate deal, the investors come out of the woodwork. We'll talk more about finding a deal later.

Your investor partner could be a family member, friend, neighbor, your dentist, doctor, or somebody you meet through networking. Talk about what you're looking to do with everyone you know and go to events/seminars/workshops where real estate investors hang out. Ask people what kind of return they would be happy with – 7%? 8%? 10%? What would motivate them to invest? Then your job is to find the property that can generate that return. Always have a written contract when it comes to any business partnership, especially when working with family or friends! It can be easy to just go on a handshake when you know someone well, but you need to make sure both of you remember the agreement in the same way years down the road. For that, you need a written record that spells out specifically what each party is entitled to and is responsible for. Who will pay for maintenance and repairs? What happens if there is a vacancy? When will you sell the property? What is the exit strategy? How will profits be divided? Try to think of everything that could happen ahead of time so there is less room for arguments and problems in the future. If things go well, this could be a joint venture for multiple properties. Keep things clear and transparent at all times.

- If you are a licensed agent, you can use your commission as part of the down-payment. Write it into the offer to prevent any misunderstandings later. Transparency is always best. Check with your broker to see if your office will allow you to keep the whole commission when purchasing your own properties.

- Start saving now. If you haven't already, start now. Investing with your own money gives you more control and more profits. You could save for the entire down payment or a portion of it and supplement with one of the methods described above. Wealthy people pay themselves first. In other words, set aside funds to invest from your income before you pay bills or spend on discretionary things. Look at your income and expenses and set aside as much as you can! 5%, 10% 25%, more? That is up to you. But the more you can save now, the wealthier you will be in the future. Think like Warren Buffet. He looks at each dollar not just as a dollar but as the potential for thousands of dollars in the future. By spending that dollar instead of investing it, he knows he is not just losing the dollar but he is losing the future value of that money. When you think like that, you will be much less inclined to spend frivolously, not out of greed but out of the knowledge that your money can do a lot more for you and others when invested. *Automate* your saving so you don't have to think about it. You can have your bank do this for you, or you could use an app such as Acorns, Qapital or Mint.

- Don't let the down-payment stop you. With some creativity and hard work, you can do this. The cash you use for your down-payment will start working for you the moment you invest it into an income property. Your hard work will pay off in dividends down the line!

12

HOW DO I FIND AN INVESTMENT PROPERTY?

*"Every person who invests in well-selected
real estate in a growing section of a
prosperous community adopts the surest and
safest method of becoming independent, for
real estate is the basis of wealth."*

—*Theodore Roosevelt*

This is where the rubber meets the road! As I mentioned before when talking about flips, finding a deal is usually harder than finding money to invest. However, you don't necessarily need to find a "deal." Due to the short-term nature of flipping a house, it is best to buy 10% below market value to leave room for a profit that is worth the inherent risk. When buying a property to hold for the long-term, however, buying at market value is OK because you have time for the property to appreciate. Of course, you never want to overpay. That's why it's important to know the market, and a good agent is invaluable here. They will do a market analysis for the property based on the recent, comparable sales. They will also know local market trends like the back of their hand.

Now that you have saved up your hard-earned money and are ready to put it to work, you want to make sure you have an excellent team around you to help guide you through the process and minimize mistakes. I've already discussed consulting a CPA, financial planner and mortgage broker. A trusted real estate agent and attorney are also critical players on your team. It bears elaborating on this point because so many buyers seem to disregard the importance of having a great buyer agent. Some believe that they will save money by going direct to the listing agent. However, this is flawed thinking. The listing agent is legally and ethically bound to protect the seller's best interests. They are professionally trained and experienced in negotiation and contractually bound to *negotiate for the seller and against you, the buyer.* Furthermore, a listing contract stipulates the total commission the seller owes the listing agent as well as the buyer agency fee. Unless they have made a special arrangement, the listing agent will keep the entire commission if there is no buyer agent because they have to do more work when there is no buyer agent involved. They are facilitating the transaction on your end as well as representing the seller.

In other words, there is no guarantee whatsoever that you will save money by waiving your right to use a buyer agent. In fact, it's more likely that you are costing yourself money because you do not have a professional negotiator in your corner protecting your interests. When there are hundreds of thousands of dollars on the line, it's not always easy to keep your cool in negotiations. That's why having a third party, professional negotiator who can stay objective is so important.

Lastly, you don't know what you don't know. We Realtors are immersed in our industry every day. Leverage your team so you don't have to know everything! Sit down and talk to your agent before you sign a contract. Make sure you have good rapport, they know what they are talking about, and you understand how they work. DO sign a service agreement. Why? Because if you are not committed to your agent, then why should they commit their time and energy to you? Remember, agents work on 100% commission. They can only make you a priority if they know that when you purchase a property, their efforts will be rewarded. If they ran around for every Tom, Dick or Harriet who said, "I want to invest, let me know when you see a deal," their kids would starve. So, sign up and *motivate* them to work for you. Buyer agency is free to a buyer because the seller pays the commission. And there is no obligation to buy. If you decide not to buy or if you want to fire your agent, you can. Just cancel the contract. You can have that written into the buyer agency agreement if it's not already there. When your buyer agent knows they will be compensated for their efforts, they will go above and beyond for you. For example, on our team, we door-knock and make proactive phone calls to neighborhoods to find off-market sellers for our buyers. This is hard and tedious work, and we can only bring these opportunities to our clients who have signed a service agreement.

Having a solid team around you will serve you well from your first investment property to your last. There are so many decisions that have to be made, big and small. It will benefit you greatly to be able to make a call to the appropriate person on your team and get a quick, no BS answer. When choosing an agent, inquire whether they have a solid network of professionals such as a CPA, a contractor and attorneys that you can lean into. Because your agent lives and breathes real estate every day, they should have strong relationships with these key players because they consistently send them business. In return, those professionals will respond quicker to calls from the agent and their clients, knowing that not just one piece of business but an entire stream of referral clients is at stake. My contractor is SO reliable. He responds quickly, gives free estimates and always sticks to his quotes. This is priceless in my business when so many contractors don't pick up the phone, don't show up, or low-ball quotes only to add on costs later. Deals happen fast, and a reliable team helps you confidently take action.

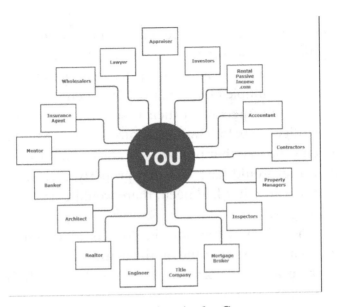

Figure 9. You Are At the Center

We had some buyers who kept getting beat out in bidding wars. At the time, bidding wars were the norm in our market. Any well-priced listing was getting multiple offers and the prices kept getting bid up. Understandably, the fear of overpaying prevented our buyers from winning the bidding wars, and they were getting frustrated. So we encouraged them to look at some listings that had been sitting on the market for a while. Buyers instinctively overlook these properties assuming that something is wrong with them. However, in most cases, they are simply overpriced.

Our Team Buyer Specialist, Chelsea Gelinas, found a property that was perfect for these clients (in a great area that they were not initially considering, I might add), and she was able to negotiate the sellers down to a mutually agreeable price. Without the pressure of a multiple offer situation, our clients were able to have an inspection at their leisure and do all their due diligence before signing a Purchase and Sale. Oh, and, by the way, they probably got the property for less than they would have had that property been priced right because if it had been, there would have been a bidding war!

The moral of the story is: don't overlook properties that have been sitting on the market. In fact, think of them as an opportunity. It's natural to think that something is wrong with them because they have been passed over by everybody else, yet most often they are just overpriced. Pricing is so important in marketing a listing that you could say these homes are not really on the market at all. However, if the seller is motivated enough, they may very well accept a lower offer. The advantage for you, the buyer, is little or no competition. You may have to make ten offers on these stale listings to get one accepted. You have to find the motivated sellers. Work with your agent to identify these opportunities. Crunch your numbers and decide what price works for you. Make your offer and see where it goes. Do not fall in love with the property! If the seller is not motivated to lower their price, just move on to the next one.

Study the market. One of the first things your buyer agent will do is set you up with an automatic

MLS (Multiple Listing Service) search. This is the main database for real estate listings and is only available through a licensed agent or broker. You will receive daily emails alerting you to all the new listings or price-changed listings that match your criteria. Go and view some of these homes. Start by touring open houses. Nothing compares to visiting homes in person and scouting neighborhoods to help you learn what's out there and what you can get for your money. Get out there and touch some properties in person and you will develop an intuitive sense of the market.

After you have seen some homes, figure out what your financial criteria are for your purchase. If this is going to be your home as well as an investment (owner occupied), it may not be possible to have positive cash flow immediately. In this case, you need to decide what is your target monthly payment after factoring in your rental income and expenses. The expenses you will need to factor in are:

- Principal and Interest (P&I) – otherwise known as your mortgage payment
- Property taxes
- Home Insurance (these four are otherwise known as PITI)
- Repair fund contributions for routine maintenance and emergency repairs
- Condo association fees if applicable
- 10% vacancy rate

Compare these expenses to your actual or antici-pated rental income as you browse properties, and this will help you focus your search on areas where you can get to your desired number.

If this property is a full-on investment, i.e., you will not be living there, then you will most likely want a positive cash flow as soon as you take ownership. However, some investors are OK with breaking even because the tenants are paying down the mortgage, and they are accumulating equity. It's a forced savings plan. In a strong market, the rent will soon increase, giving you a positive cash flow in the future. It's up to you to decide what you are comfortable with.

In either case, make sure that you calculate the expenses above and remember to factor in a 10% vacancy rate into the income. Even in highly desirable areas, you could end up with a vacancy, and it's always best to be conservative. It will be helpful to use an Excel spreadsheet to plug in numbers and quickly ana-lyze deals to help you make fast decisions. There are lots of sample spreadsheets available online. But ulti-mately, you are the only one who can say what works for you and your goals. So put some thought into that and create or adapt a spreadsheet that works for you. Having a clear understanding of what you are look-ing for will save you a bunch of wasted time looking at properties that don't fit your parameters.

I mentioned before that you don't necessarily have to find a "below market deal" unless it's a short-term flip. If you are holding the property for 2 years or more, then it's more important to find a good property in a good location than to buy for less than market value. The virtues of a good piece of real estate will outweigh the upfront dollars you might save by buying something just because it's cheap. Many people come to me and say they want to buy a foreclosure. Why? Because they have heard they can find a deal by buying a foreclosure. However, keep in mind the following:

- If an owner hasn't been paying their mortgage, it's more than likely they haven't been paying for maintenance either. Therefore, many foreclosed homes have a lot of deferred maintenance and/or need costly structural or mechanical repairs, which could end up costing you far more in the long run than buying a non-distressed property. There may be other hidden costs like tax liens or unpaid utility bills that the buyer could be responsible for.
- You will likely find yourself in competition with contractors, developers and cash buyers who will bid up the price and make offers without contingencies for inspections and financing. If you are a first-time investor, you probably need those protections, so it will be difficult for you to compete unless you are contractor.

Personally, I would rather pay a little more and know what I am getting into than buy a foreclosed home at an auction and not have the opportunity to inspect the home and run the risk of getting in over my head.

If you are looking for a property to flip, aim to buy the property 10% or more below market value. Besides looking at stale or expired listings, here are some other techniques for finding deals:

- FSBO's – For Sale By Owners. Sometimes, home sellers choose to sell their homes "off-market" or by owner in order to save on Realtor fees. The irony is that investors prey on these sellers knowing that they will have less competition than on the market and may be able to get a deal. In the meantime, regular buyers will tend to avoid for-sale-by-owners because it feels a little sketchy not having the protection of a licensed brokerage handling the sale. FSBO's are also notoriously hard to negotiate with due to their subjectivity and attachment to their properties. However, there are some out there who are motivated, so it is worth checking out sites like Zillow and Craigslist to see if you can get into an off-market property.

- Cold-calling and door-knocking. These are techniques that super-motivated Realtors use to turn up listings for their business. You could also use them to find a property OR hire an agent who will do it on your behalf. We routinely do this for our clients. Perhaps there is a particular neighborhood you would love to purchase in. Nothing is stopping you from knocking on doors around there and asking people if they know anyone who wants to sell a home. Most people are flattered to know they live in a desirable neighborhood, but there are some cranky-pants out there, so make sure you phrase it as "Do you know anyone…" not "Do you want to sell?" so as not to offend anyone. My team and I have had several successes matching our buyers with off-market homes. It's a numbers game. We dedicate a chunk of time almost every day looking for sellers for our buyers and buyers for our sellers. And occasionally, it works out! When it does, it's truly a win-win. The buyer finds a home before the rest of the world knows about it, which typically saves the buyer money. The seller doesn't have to deal with a lot of showings and aggravation with putting the home on the market and saves money on commission because it's a direct buyer.

- Let everyone you know that you are looking for an investment property. Talk to people and encourage them to bring you opportunities. Let them know you will look at anything; they don't have to screen them first. You are not looking to steal a property from someone. It's only a good deal if it's a win-win as described above. If the seller for whatever reason does not want to put the home on the market, you can help them and yourself at the same time. By the way, you could also find a partner by having these kinds of conversations.

- There may be someone in your network who would be a good "bird-dog." A bird-dog is someone who finds opportunities and brings them to you, sometimes for a small fee. This person could be a handyman, a contractor, an appraiser, an insurance adjuster, or anyone who sees a lot of properties by virtue of their work or just as a hobby. An estate attorney or bailer could be a good resource, as morbid as it might sound. You may get lucky talking to a mail person for the neighborhood you're interested in. They could tip you off to a property where the mail has been building up for months. Note: if you come across an abandoned home, I have a system for locating long-lost heirs. Contact me at careyteamcg@gmail.com and I will walk you through it.

You could also go as far as doing a direct mail marketing campaign. However, unless you have the time and resources to make this a consistent effort, it's probably not worthwhile. Direct mail will be pretty hit or miss, unless you dedicate hours a day stuffing envelopes or hire someone to do it for you. The return on direct mail is typically around 1%. Your time is better spent looking on the market where you know the seller is motivated and ready to sell and the pertinent information is presented to you in a nice, clean package. Your valuable time can be spent visiting the properties, running your analyses and consulting with your team on securing a fantastic property that will bring you long-term wealth rather than chasing unmotivated sellers. However, I have recently come across an app called Deal Machine, which makes it very easy to mail custom pieces to owners of properties you find that appear to be abandoned, distressed or neglected. You simply snap a photo of the property on the phone and the app locates the address using GPS, and searches public records for the owner's information. You click to send them a postcard with the property photo on it making it more likely that they will look at it. The probability of finding a deal this way is higher than send mass mailings: more like 1 out of 200.

If you enjoy the thrill of the chase, perhaps you should consider becoming an agent yourself! You could find deals not only for yourself but have the ability to shop them around as well and earn commissions. One great thing about real estate: there is no ceiling. Sales can complement a real estate investing career nicely. For example, you are the first to know about your own listings, so you have the first opportunity to buy them. Working in the market every day will give you an intimate knowledge of it. Thirdly, agents often tell each other about their new listings as they are prepping them for presentation to the public. Around 15% of properties are sold before they hit the MLS. (One more reason to work with a plugged-in agent unless you are one yourself!)

Disclaimer: Because real estate is such an easy profession to get licensed in and so potentially lucrative, it is also *very* competitive. You will need to do what it takes every day to build a database, build your reputation and continually serve your clients, past and present. As the Productivity Coach in our office, I train and coach our new agents, and I have to say that the biggest misconception new agents have is that it's easy money. Yes, the initial barrier to entry – getting a license – is relatively easy. It requires 48 hours coursework and a score of 70% or higher on the licensing exam. However, building a business from scratch on 100% commission is not easy. Many people approach real estate sales with a part time mentality, thinking they can do it "in their free time." Let me just be really blunt: it rarely works out. Yes, your hours are flexible to some degree, yet you still have to consistently put in a lot of time and hustle to generate business, and then you have to serve your clients. You will have to be available when they are available.

Therefore, to make it worthwhile, you will almost certainly find that you not only have to work full-time, you have to work *overtime*, at least in the beginning.

If you enjoy challenges and are genuinely interested in a real estate career, I would love to talk with you about your goals and answer your questions. If you are willing to work hard and do what it takes, real estate offers you the opportunity to earn as much money as you want. Furthermore, at Keller Williams, our motto is "It's not about the money, it's about being the best you can be." When you grow as a person, your business follows. I'm always looking to grow and challenge myself in new ways. In my opinion, that's the best part about being a real estate agent – you never stop learning and growing!

13

WHEN IS THE BEST TIME TO BUY?

"Don't wait to buy real estate. Buy real estate and wait."

—*Robert G. Allen*

"When is the best time to buy?" I get this question a lot, as if there is some magic date or time when deals fall from the sky! Wouldn't that be great? Obviously, the market cycles up and down, and it's always good to know where we are in the cycle when buying. If you are able to buy when the market is down, that's ideal. However, if you hold real estate long-term, it's almost always a good time to buy because over time, the market always trends up. More importantly, if you are getting a positive cash flow from your property, then appreciation is just the icing on the cake. The ebbs

Figure 10. New Housing Starts

and flows of the market will even out over the years. Waiting for the market to tank could mean you are losing out on that positive cash flow in the interim, and no one knows when the market will dip. The best indicator, however, goes back to the most basic law of economics: Supply and Demand. Home prices go up because supply is lower than demand. Homes prices go down when supply is higher than demand.

When I started my career as a real estate agent in 2010, foreclosures glutted the market. Buyers were super scared to buy anything because they didn't know where the bottom was. My listings would sit for months, and price reductions were commonplace. I heard a famous real estate coach, Brian Buffini, talking about where the market was headed in 2012. He said he had been watching "new starts" – the number of new homes being built. For the few years prior to 2012, new starts had been close to zero because the buyer demand was very low. However, after several years with no new construction happening, the population still growing and the investors buying up all the foreclosures at rock-bottom prices, the inventory was beginning to dry up. Supply was becoming low. Therefore, he predicted that in the following year, the market would shift: the see-saw would tilt toward a sellers' market.

Sure enough, it happened just as he said. The supply began to dwindle and, there weren't so many price reductions. The prices began to stabilize and creep up. Buyers noticed and realized the bottom had already passed. Pent-up demand and increased buyer confidence meant that more buyers jumped into the fray. Demand exploded. Next thing you knew, we saw bidding wars everywhere. I still remember when I first saw an offer deadline, which is a strategy to gather all offers and allow the seller to review them before making a choice. It became very clear to me that Supply vs. Demand truly governs the market. Of course, interest rates and the economy play a role also. But nothing impacts pricing as directly as that basic law.

We could also apply that law to the seasons. When do most listings come on the market? Here in New England, it's undoubtedly the Spring. It's been a tradition for years due to the beautiful weather, spring flowers and blossoms as well as the desire of many families to move during the summer before school starts up again in the Fall. However, if you are a seller listing in the Spring, you are positioning your property against the most possible competition. Whereas, if you list your home in the dead of winter when there is very little supply, you have almost no competition. Yes, I understand there is snow, ice, and the holidays are busy. However, in a strong market like Greater Boston, people buy all year round. The main reason more don't buy in the winter is there is not much to look at. In a desirable area for a fair price, any property can sell any day of the year. In fact, sellers may get a better price during the "off-season" because supply is lower. Bottom line: the best time to buy an investment property was 20 years ago. The second best time: today.

14

HOW DO I AVOID BUYING THE MONEY PIT?

"Risk comes from not knowing what you're doing."

—*Warren Buffet*

Figure 11. The Money Pit

Tom Hanks was in the prime of his youth in the movie **The Money Pit**. He was your everyday guy trying to do well in life by buying a fixer-upper, only to be confounded at every turn by this lemon of a house that literally fell apart at the seams and led to many a hilarious pratfall. The movie is so funny and relatable because it taps into an underlying fear many of us have around buying a property. All that money, representing years of hard work, poured into a property that represents our hopes and dreams for our future. And then, the thing sucks the soul right out of us just as it sucks the money from our bank account right down the drain.

How do you avoid this scenario? Have an inspection. Choose a highly reputable inspector to help you examine the property before you sign a P&S. In a competitive situation such as a bidding war or an auction, you may not have this opportunity. You may be up against developers and very experienced investors and developers who will not need to do an inspection, so you will not have a fighting chance if you make your offer contingent on it. That's why, personally, as a first time (or even second time) buyer, I would not advise jumping into a bidding situation where you cannot have an inspection. Go the safer route and do your due diligence. You may not get a "deal" necessarily, but in the long-term, you'll be better off. When buying an investment property to hold over 10, 20, or 30 years, it's OK to buy at market value. The income is what is most important here, not necessarily the equity. That's just icing on the cake.

An inspector will tell you what the home needs now, if anything, and what to expect for repairs and maintenance in the foreseeable future. KEEP IN MIND: the vast majority of homes on the market are resales (not new construction), and there are always going to be things that need to be done. It's easy to get overwhelmed when you see a laundry list of items on the inspection report. For the purpose of the purchase, focus in on major repairs: things that are urgent, safety-related, and/or costly (over $5k), such as structural or mechanical defects.

Ask your inspector which items are major using the criteria above. If something may or may not need addressed five or more years down the road, it's probably not a reason to withdraw the offer or to renegotiate the price. That's just the reality of owning a house. Eventually it will need a roof, and you will need to replace the water heater, and so on. But if the foundation or the structure of the house needs attention, or the mechanics (plumbing, electrical, heating) are defective, then you should determine what the issue is, if it's fixable and how much it would cost. Your agent can then talk to the seller and (assuming it wasn't already disclosed prior to your offer), ask them to make the repair before the closing or give you a credit to do the repair yourself. Depending on the situation and relevant factors such as the originally agreed upon price and the heat of the market, you may negotiate a new price or a credit with the seller, have them fix the problem, or walk away from the deal entirely. As long as you have an inspection contingency, you are protected.

If you do find yourself in a highly competitive situation as a first-time buyer, you could always have an inspection without making the offer contingent upon the outcome. What that means is that you risk your first deposit if you decide to withdraw your offer after it's accepted. In our market, the first deposit is typically $1000. However, if not having a contingency for inspection wins you the property without overpaying for it, you may decide that it's worth risking the $1000. If you do this, make sure the offer says, "Buyer will have inspection for informational purposes only before the P&S" so that only your first deposit and not your second deposit is at risk. We did this when we bought our two-family. It was 2015, and the market was super hot. We put in a full-price offer with no inspection contingency because we knew that if another offer came in higher, we would have to increase our bid. We offered the seller exactly what they wanted, and they took it right away. Sometimes, in a hot market, you have to be bold. If you can, have your contractor walk through the property before you make your offer. They know what to look for and can tell you if there are any major repairs to be done. Keep in mind, neither the contractor nor the inspector can see through walls. Always factor a 10% contingency buffer into any renovation budget just in case of surprises.

Now I would like to touch upon some frequently asked questions about real estate investing. Most (if not all) things in real estate are negotiable, and there are many grey areas. If you need more specific answers, give me a call at 617-791-4882 or email me at careyteamcg@gmail.com.

Tips on Buying Real Estate

A. How do I structure an offer? This depends largely on whether or not it's a competitive situation. Make sure you're protected by the contingencies in the offer. At the same time, in a competitive market, you may choose to take on more of the transactional risk in order to get your offer accepted. Going back to finding overpriced properties, the beauty of shopping these listings is that you will have less competition because other buyers are overlooking them. Therefore, in these cases you could get away with more contingencies in the offer, whereas in a bidding war situation, you want to have as few as possible.

B. How do I form a power team of professionals to help me buy and maintain my property? Reliable professionals are worth their weight in gold – contractor, plumber, electrician, attorney, CPA and lender, to name a few. Talk to your Realtor. If you have an excellent Realtor, they are likely the hub in the wheel of home and financial services and therefore will have all of these contacts at their fingertips. Also, if they regularly give referrals to these folks, the service providers may give priority to their clients. Meet with these people and let them know you are a professional investor (a potential repeat client). Ask them about their business, their experience, and how they communicate with clients. Do they take an educational approach with their clients? Ideally, you want someone with experience who has the heart of a teacher and will take the time to walk you through the finer points. Do you connect with them on a personal level? Always partner with people you like and trust.

C. Should I buy a property that needs work? Yes! However, look for properties that have "good bones" Look for the diamonds in the rough that only need cosmetics, not major repairs, unless of course you are a contractor.

D. What should I expect as a landlord? I strongly recommend keeping your rents slightly less than market to ensure tenants who stay and take care of the property. Take care of your tenants, and they will take care of you. However, don't let your rents fall too far behind the market value. Make small incremental increases every two or three years, $100/month, for example. That way, you don't have to suddenly make a large increase after many years, which could shock the tenant and force them to leave. If and when you sell your property, the rental income will affect the property value, so it's important to keep pace with the market. A great property manager is worth their weight in gold. Talk to your agent and network with other investors to get referrals.

Selling an investment property is a subject in and of itself, and there are many complexities.

Tips on Selling Real Estate

A. Plan your exit strategy when you buy – the more options the better. Depending on the market and your life circumstances, you could rent, sell, or move in. If you need some but not all of the cash out, rather than selling, you could refinance or get a home equity line of credit (HELOC).

B. Be aware of your future plans vs. market cycles. We've all heard the rule of thumb: buy low, sell high. Historically, market cycles last for about ten years. If you hold a property for 10 years or more, you will ride out dips in the market. We have seen over the last ten years the market bounce back even after the great housing crash of 2007-2008. But if you may only own the property for 5 years, you'll want to be reasonably sure you are not buying at the peak of the market.

C. Selling by owner vs. with an agent. Research shows that FSBO's leave $ on the table. Do you remember when you wanted a deal? You shopped FSBO's, right? But if you're selling, don't trip over dollars to pick up dimes. When savvy buyers want a deal on a car, electronics or jewelry, they shop eBay and Craigslist: they go directly to the seller to save money. The same principle applies in real estate, but all too often the seller is inexperienced and will lose out to the buyer. You and the buyer cannot save the same dollar. On the other hand, when a consumer walks into Long's Jewelry, they are prepared to pay a higher price for a product than they might pay through an auction or on the black market because they know they are buying through a reputable merchant. Likewise, when a buyer works through a real estate broker, they understand they are paying fair market prices, and that's fine because they have the peace of mind of working with a licensed and insured professional.

D. Renovate or sell as-is? While any property will sell at the right price, there are often ways to boost your property's value with a few simple strategies. The first rule of thumb is to simply de-clutter. Even the tidiest person could pare down the extra stuff in their home. If you are moving, just start packing! Pack anything you won't need in the next couple of months. Clear out bulky or unnecessary furniture. After that, work with whatever budget you have to do minor repairs and cosmetic touches around the house. Paint is cheap and goes a long way. Make the home feel as fresh, spacious and organized as possible. Working within your budget, improve the curb appeal and/or refresh the kitchens and baths. Ask a trusted real estate agent for advice. All real estate is local, and your agent will know specifically what most buyers are looking for in your area at any given time. Broader buyer appeal means more money in your pocket.

E. When you're ready to trade up your current investment property for a bigger, better one, you will want to learn more about 1031 tax deferred exchanges. This amazing tool allows you to defer capital gains taxes indefinitely. Talk to your CPA and your real estate agent for a referral to a 1031 exchange intermediary.

F. Condo conversion – in the Greater Boston market where there is not much land available, condo conversion has boomed in the past few years. This has inspired many multi-family owners to consider doing it themselves. However, while it may look easy when the developers do it, this process could take two or more years and cost hundreds of thousands of dollars. I implore you, talk to a real estate professional to get expert advice. While there is potential for great profit, I've seen too many sellers come to me with a finished product that could have been much more marketable and profitable if they had talked to me before and during the process. Sometimes, the seller would have been better off selling as a multi-unit than investing hundreds of thousands of dollars into a sub-par product.

G. Maximize your value – Maintain, maintain, maintain. Do not defer maintenance. Make small upgrades every year so repairs don't accumulate. Repairs and maintenance on income properties are tax deductible. With income properties, the resale value is all about the financials. It's not so much about having a pretty house as having a house that will bring in good rents and will not cost the next owner much money to upkeep. Unless it's a luxury rental, there is no need to go top of line with materials. Focus on practicality and durability. If you have questions on specific upgrades, talk to an experienced rental agent or property manager in your area. Also, make small increases in rent every two years keeping in pace with the market.

15

NOW IT'S YOUR TURN

"Your diamonds are not in far distant mountains or in yonder seas; they are in your own backyard, if you but dig for them."

—*Russell H. Conwell, Acres of Diamonds*

One thing I've learned on my journey is that "having it all" does not necessarily equate to having a picture-perfect life. As much as I adore my kids and enjoy my career, sometimes I look up from the whirlwind that is my daily life and I wonder, why in God's name did I bring this upon myself? The soccer games, the gymnastics classes, the networking events, the negotiations with clients and with the kids – it's downright exhausting.

Then I take a few moments to breathe in and out, relax, and try to remember that this is what 'having it all' really is. It's not about being perfect, it's about being on a path to reaching the goals that you set out for yourself. It's about having balance in your life. Balance is the result of two equal and opposing pressures, such as work and family. Instead of looking to relieve the pressure, I have come to realize that the pressures of work and family are actually what keep me balanced. If I'm feeling off-balance, like when I've worked too many long days in a row, I take an afternoon off to see my kids, plan a family trip or volunteer at their school.

I am constantly adjusting and counter-balancing. And that's OK. I choose to embrace the chaos! Let's face it, there's plenty of chaos out there, and you need figure out how to deal with it rather than deny that it is there. That's the beauty of it. Happiness is in the journey, the struggle, the adventure. For me, happiness is giving my kids a hug before school, reading a story at bedtime, taking family trips and showing my kids that a mother can also have a career. And then I've got my life with my husband. When we know that we're making progress, all the daily ups and downs can be put into perspective.

There are times when I feel I'm doing it all wrong. I get stressed and scream at my kids, and that's OK. I love this quote by Reese Witherspoon: "If you don't scream at your kids, you're not spending enough time with them." That's the truth. Yet my kids inspire me even more than they exhaust me. I will go to the ends of the earth for them. Sometimes, I yearn for the day when I can watch Netflix all day, but in all honesty, that would probably drive me crazy after an hour or two. Although it's counter-intuitive, research shows people are actually happiest while in pursuit of a goal, not at the finish line.

Everything happens for a reason. There is a reason that you are reading this book right now. I believe that the universe provides you with all the opportunities you need to obtain your dreams and wishes. You only need to be open to them. Sit back and let them in. You are indeed standing on your own acres of diamonds. If you have been searching for a way to secure your own future or your family's, real estate investing could be a vehicle for doing just that. If you crave stability in an uncertain world, then turning your income into assets could give you peace of mind. If you are anxious about the next wave of layoff's, the next economic downturn, or new technologies like Artificial Intelligence doing away with your job, remember this: people will always need homes.

While the population steadily increases, they are not making any more land. That's a pretty good indicator that residential real estate will continue to increase in value. Personally, I love it that real estate can be both a home and an investment. It is a safe haven, literally and figuratively.

Open up your thinking, find a way, and take action. I've heard some "experts" say that Millennials feel that they are privileged and don't want to work, but that's not my experience. People are people, and everyone wants a better future for themselves and their kids. That's always been the case, and it always will be.

Real estate is one vehicle to make that a reality.

You deserve to have your piece of the American Dream. You have the power to determine your future. However, it's not enough just to read or listen to information about real estate. You have to surround yourself with the right people who are doing it. Find a mentor and build a team. I am walking the walk, and for some of you, it would be great to do it right along with you. I already offer my guidance every step of the way to new agents at our office. Why not others who aren't professionals in the business? Why not you?

No matter what you decide, I urge you to get started today! Remember what they say about the best time to plant a tree.

When you invest in real estate, time is on your side.

ABOUT THE AUTHOR

Carey Gatto was born in Northern Ireland and lived in England, upstate New York and Maine before attending Boston College. She graduated from BC in 2001, produced several independent films and earned a Master's degree in film production from Emerson College. She married Joe Gatto, and they moved to LA where Carey worked at a talent agency in Beverly Hills. Carey and Joe bought their first condo while she was pregnant with their first child. They renovated it and sold it a year later for a profit to move back to Boston.

Carey became addicted to real estate because of the income potential and lifestyle it offered. When the Gattos moved back East in 2010, she immediately studied for and passed her real estate test and started building her business. In 2015, Carey joined Keller Williams Realty in Cambridge.

A natural born leader, Carey soon developed the skills that enabled her to become the Productivity Coach in the 100 agent office, where she mentors new agents and helps them succeed. She also takes real estate investors under her wing so that they can achieve their life goals. She is rapidly becoming known as the "go to" real estate coach for the Millennial generation. With her stellar track record and growing number of clients who rave about her services, she is a living example of success in real estate while also leading a balanced family life.

"It's not as hard as many people think," Carey tells everyone. "You really can have it all with real estate."

Carey is available to answer your questions. You can give her a call at 617-791-4882 or email her at careyteamcg@gmail.com.

CPSIA information can be obtained
at www.ICGtesting.com
Printed in the USA
FSHW011008161119
64119FS